Language:
The Big Picture

Language:
The Big Picture

Peter Sharpe

continuum

KH

Continuum International Publishing Group

The Tower Building
11 York Road
London, SE1 7NX

80 Maiden Lane
Suite 704, New York
NY 10038

www.continuumbooks.com

British Library Cataloguing-in-Publication Data
A catalogue record for this book is available from the British Library.

ISBN: 978-0-8264-9814-4 (Hardback)
         978-0-8264-9815-1 (Paperback)

Library of Congress Cataloging-in-Publication Data
The Publisher has applied for CIP data.

Typeset by Newgen Imaging Systems Pvt Ltd, Chennai, India
Printed and bound in Great Britain by MPG Books, Cornwall

10/5/09

For all the students
who made my ten years of teaching well spent,
but especially for
Gai Qi, Ma Yunlan, Fan Yinguang, Sato Akihito,
Do Minh Khai, Ming Yi, Thida Kyi, Gen Shun, Ren Na,
Nozu Shoko, Yoshikawa Yuki
and my good friend
Mamiko

Contents

Introduction

What is Language?

The exact nature and workings of language seem to have eluded a totally satisfactory explanation. Why should this be so? Is it so huge a phenomenon that it cannot be neatly reduced to a theoretical model? Is it too complicated and hopelessly tangled into the fabric of culture to be teased out and made clear for all to see? Or, are we so utterly confined within it that we find it impossible to step outside and view its boundaries objectively?

The answers to these questions will take us on a journey across the territory of several disciplines. We shall discover that the problems posed by language are central, not only to linguistics, but many other fields. But before beginning, let's look at the advantages of viewing language from several perspectives, how the chapters will be ordered and clear up an ambiguity.

The Viewpoint Problem

The Swiss Ferdinand de Saussure (1857–1913) is generally acknowledged as the founder of linguistics. He defined its object of enquiry as the **sign** (word). At the same time, he recognized that this entity was problematic. A word could be a sound, a written symbol, an expression of an idea, an equivalent of another word, a derivative of an earlier form, etc. Whichever view you took, it always seemed to affect the outcome. If you were interested in sound, the study became phonetic. If you were interested in how words combine to make sentences, the study became grammatical, and so on. Saussure also noticed that no single viewpoint seemed to have a natural priority: language had many different faces. He called this 'the viewpoint problem'.

Among language's different faces, he saw four that formed twin aspects. These dualities were:

(i) the sounds of speech are not just sounds, they create acoustic impressions that need to be interpreted by listeners;
(ii) sound is also the instrument of thought, it combines with an idea to form a complex psychological unit;
(iii) speech has both an individual and a social aspect and neither can exist without the other; and
(iv) speech always implies both an established system and an evolution – 'at every moment it is an existing institution and a product of the past' (Saussure 1916: 8).

It is clear that the investigation of these dualities involves several disciplines – psychology, anthropology and philosophy to name but a few. This is why a single disciplinary approach is doomed from the outset: it can only result in a particular view of language, one circumscribed by subject boundaries. To see the big picture, language must be viewed from several vantage points. Some details, of course, will have to be sacrificed to achieve this panoramic view, but if the end result is a fuller understanding of the true scope of language it will be worth it.

The Study of Language

To better understand the viewpoint problem, let's imagine a building so vast that it cannot be viewed in its entirety from any angle. Not even from the air can all of it be seen because it has subterranean floors. It also has an irregular shape which, to make matters worse, is changing slowly over time. This building represents language. Only one of its wings is devoted to its scientific study, it's called '**Linguistics**'. It has several entrances, but the following names adorn the main doorways – Sound, Structure and Meaning.

Peeping into the doorway marked 'Sound' one would notice three corridors leading away from the reception area. One, named **phonetics,** studies the place and manner of articulation of the smallest unit of sound, the **phoneme**. The adjoining corridor is **phonology**. Its study concerns the system that the sounds of languages form. The last corridor is **prosody** which studies tone, pitch and stress that are placed upon the sounds of language.

Someone entering through the doorway marked 'Structure' would notice that the floors have been arranged according to different **levels of analysis**. The ground floor specializes in the study of the atoms of word structure, the **morpheme**. This is the smallest functioning unit of a word; for example, the {un-}, {touch}, {-able}, {-s} of 'untouchables'. The first floor is given to the study of **lexemes** (for example, 'go' is the lexeme for 'goes', 'gone', 'went', etc.). The next floor studies **sentences** which are defined as the largest grammatical unit. There are also adjoining floors, specializing in a range of other linguistic matters.

Stepping through the doorway marked 'Meaning', one is faced by a bewildering choice of corridors. We had best leave **semantics** (the study of meaning) till later.

Stepping outside and looking up, we see a pinnacle. It is there that the theorists work. It is their job to explain how the three different aspects of language work together. To date, theories have tended to be either **formalist** or **functionalist**. Formalist theories believe language has an abstract form that lies behind its outward structure. They view this underlying form as the core or essence of language. Functionalists are more concerned with the social uses to which language is put. They investigate the structure of language in terms of its functions. At the moment, formalist theories are in the ascendant, but the history of linguistics shows that the pendulum of satisfactory explanations tends to swing back and forth between the two.

Although it is sometimes forgotten, the forms our curiosity takes about things is described in a dusty tome deep in the basement of the building. Written by a Greek philosopher called Aristotle (384–322 BC), it identifies a fourfold scheme of causation, four questions that we might want answered about anything. They are:

(1) We may be curious about what something is made of, its matter or material cause.
(2) We may be curious about the form (or structure or shape) that its matter takes, its formal cause.
(3) We may be curious about its beginning, how it got started, or its efficient cause.
(4) We may be curious about its purpose or goal or end, sometimes translated in English, somewhat controversially, as 'final cause'.

Aristotle's classification still holds true today; in fact, it forms the framework within which nearly all scientific research is conducted.

There are many scholars who examine the matter, or substance, of language – its sounds. There are also many who research the formal cause, the **syntax** or structure of language – how its words combine meaningfully to form sentences. While there are fewer involved in the study of its efficient cause, or origin, there are many who emphasize the purposes, or **functions**, of language.

From the above, we can see that not only have we inherited the general framework of rational enquiry from the thinkers of ancient Greece, but that within linguistics – the discipline most directly concerned with the study of language – subject boundaries and levels of analysis have been established. This marks the starting point of our knowledge. Every discipline has boundaries and levels of analysis, and they are there for good reasons – to limit the scope of investigation so as to enable specialization. However, boundaries and divisions can introduce an element of artificiality that prevents the full scope of the phenomenon under investigation from being seen. This is another good reason to adopt a broader approach to the study of language.

Order of Chapters

In the same way that an artist will view an object from several positions, we shall proceed in a similar fashion, pausing at various vantage points to see what different faces language reveals.

The first chapter examines what is known about the origins of language since this seems the most natural starting point. The second chapter asks if language is exclusive to humans and answers affirmatively by arguing that there would be no language without our kind of consciousness. The third describes how language changes with time. The fourth how language varies across cultures since so much of what we say (including what I am writing now) is predetermined by the issues of the social reality into which we chance to be born. The fifth looks at how linguists approach the study of language and, in particular, how the American linguist Noam Chomsky (b. 1928) has influenced the direction and aims of linguistics. The sixth asks what criteria linguistic theories must fulfil to be scientific. Because of language's intricate connection to meaning, the next chapter considers various semantic theories to find out if they reveal anything of the ultimate nature of language. Chapter eight considers one of the most remarkable aspects of language, its symbolic nature. The final chapter examines what we know about how language is represented in the mind.

On route, some technical terms will be used. They will be printed in **bold** and explained in context where necessary. At times, some questions that have already been touched upon will be reconsidered from a different perspective. By doing so, it is hoped that the reader will appreciate the extent to which problems can vary according to the approach adopted. It is also my hope that non-specialists will appreciate why technical terms have to be used – it is difficult to write clearly and unambiguously without them.

The chapters progress incrementally in terms of difficulty. Not wishing to burden the reader with too much detail too quickly, the material is presented gradually. Specialists might find the earlier chapters sketchy, even superficial, but the details come later as each chapter adds more information. A summary follows each chapter accompanied by research and discussion questions for teachers who might want to use this material as a course book. Suggestions for further reading on the subject matter of each chapter are also provided.

An Ambiguity

In English, the word 'language' is ambiguous: it can mean both a system of words and grammatical rules and the spoken or written products of the use of the system. Throughout, when I use the word 'language', it will refer to both the system and its products, unless stated otherwise. Although examples will be drawn mainly from Japanese, the main purpose will be to understand language in general.

What Are the Origins of Language?

Genetic or Social?

The question as to whether human language is a genetic endowment or a social accomplishment came to the forefront of linguistic debate in the 1960s when Noam Chomsky (b. 1928) claimed that language was **species-specific** (possessed only by humans), innate (an inherited characteristic) and, most controversially, that humans were born with a specific linguistic program. The idea that humans are born with general mental learning abilities was not controversial, and most people would readily accept this as a species-specific trait of humankind. But Chomsky challenged this view by claiming that language was distinct from our other cognitive abilities and that it was genetic.

He believed that only this could explain otherwise inexplicable phenomena. For example, how children not only acquire languages with ease, but are also able to master rules that they could not possibly have figured out for themselves because the data they are exposed to in the short time of growing up is too scant and the rules too complex. Others also drew attention to how deaf children learn sign languages, claiming this as further proof that the ability to hear or produce sounds is not a necessary condition for learning a language. Because language acquisition is not just a matter of simply building up vocabulary, but also of applying the rules that decide how vocabulary is manipulated, Chomsky was particularly interested in explaining how children could so quickly understand the principles that govern the rules of **syntax**. These rules decide how vocabulary is placed to form grammatically correct sentences.

His answer was to argue that there must be a genetically programmed **language acquisition device** that provides a closed set of common principles (sometimes referred to as **Universal Grammar**) which is then variously realized in different languages, depending on which language or languages a child is exposed to. He claimed these common principles define a number of general **parameters** (constraints) within which languages operate, but that the particular **settings** differ according to particular languages. The parameters are innately determined by the genetic make-up of humans, while the settings are variable and largely the result of different environments.

Chomsky's ideas form part of his theory of language which is called **generative grammar**. However, it is not the only explanation on offer. There are others that reflect its social uses – how it functions as a communication-system. The best known is **systemic grammar** or **systemic linguistics**. Devised by Michael Halliday (b. 1925) it addresses the same question, Why is language as it is? In stark contrast, it argues that the underlying impetus for the evolution of language was socio-cultural. This contention is not as central to his theory as its biological origins are to Chomsky's, however. The very existence of a Universal Grammar depends upon language having a genetic base.

Satisfyingly, the two theories reflect different aspects of language. The former deals with its abstract, **cognitive** aspect; that is, how it is associated with those parts of the mind that form our awareness and knowledge of the world. It attempts to find out what the forms that language takes can reveal about the mind. The latter is more concerned with language's interactive, behavioural aspect, how it functions as a social **semiotic** (a means of signalling meaning), and what syntactic forms its functions assume. Although neither theory is directly concerned with language origins, it is clear that they differ as to which aspect – inner biological or outer socio-cultural – was most important. Neither side claims one aspect is exclusively important, the difference is one of significant emphasis. With this background in mind, let's look at what is known about language's origins.

First the Body that Can Make the Sounds

Few would disagree with the common-sense statement that before humans could develop a vocal communication-system they would need to be able to make the sounds that comprise that system. Our nearest relatives, chimpanzees, cannot make the same range of sounds as we do. Our ability must, then, depend upon some anatomical difference. Leslie Aiello, professor of anthropology at University College London, singles out the low position of the **larynx** in the modern human vocal tract as the main reason. The larynx is inside the windpipe and it comprises the voice box and vocal chords that are used to vibrate lung air into sounds. Interestingly, the position of the larynx is not different at birth, but begins to descend after three months. As it does so, it opens up a space at the back of the baby's mouth just behind the tongue. Because the soft palate which is at the back of the roof of the mouth does not reach the **epiglottis** (a flap of tissue at the back of the tongue), as is the case with chimpanzees, it leaves the tongue to form a soft wall in front of the throat. It is this that allows us to make the extra sounds, producing different vowels by changing the shape of the throat and the position of the tongue. Figure 1 below gives an indication of the position of the larynx in a human.

What Caused these Changes?

Since approximately 5 million years separates us from the last common ancestor we shared with chimpanzees, Aiello writes that it would be naïve to think that modern human language developed directly from the type of communication-system that chimpanzees have. Rather, she thinks there must have been a number of important developments during that long period of time that set in motion a process that led to a much more

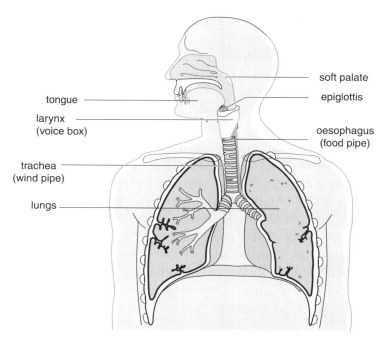

Figure 1 Position of the larynx in a human

sophisticated form of vocal communication. The accepted view is that the most important was a radical change of lifestyle; specifically, the move from a forested tree-dwelling environment to more open country.

The apes that left the chimps in the trees of the forest became ground-dwellers and, as they adapted to life on the ground, they began to walk upright. The benefit of walking on two legs is that it uses less energy and leaves the hands free to gather food, carry things, make tools and throw weapons. The celebrated natural science writer Stephen Jay Gould believes that achieving an upright posture was humankind's greatest evolutionary step and that its consequences were both far-reaching and fundamental (1980: 133).

It changed, for example, our sexual behaviour by shifting attraction from smell to the visual plane.

This move from dense forests to open wetlands required new anatomical and behavioural adaptations. For example, now it was much more difficult to hide from predators and so new strategies were needed. Some of these were only incidental to vocal communication, but others were more directly related. Three examples often cited are living and hunting in larger groups, having larger home ranges and adopting a different diet and manner of movement. It is believed that adding meat to a hitherto plant-based diet was the main cause for the anatomical changes that led to a lower larynx, smaller mouth and jaw, more rounded teeth, a muscular tongue and a less protruding face. Over time, this change to a higher quality, protein-rich diet had the following knock-on effects on early **hominids** (ape-men):

(1) they did not need to spend all day eating plants to get the necessary amount of energy to stay alive;
(2) there was no longer a need for a large stomach to digest leaves, roots and plants, and as stomachs grew smaller so posture became more upright;
(3) meat provided the protein and calories to make our brains bigger; and, finally,
(4) the enriched diet created free time which, in turn, provided the impetus for the invention of tools and more complex social grouping.

It is often thought that natural selection only applies to changes to the body. But this is not the case. Gould writes that Charles Darwin's theory of natural selection is rooted 'in the concept of *adaptation* – the idea that organisms respond to changing environments by evolving a body (form) and behaviour (function) better suited to these new circumstances' (1980: 78). Later, we shall see just how intertwined form and function are.

When Did the Changes to the Body Take Place?

When did these changes to the vocal tract and face take place? How long did the changes that turned us into humans take to evolve? Why did they take place at all? Did they take place simultaneously? And does the presence of the modern vocal tract necessarily mean that language was present? Before attempting to answer these questions, let's place them within a time frame. Figure 2 indicates the time scale of these changes.

The connections between the various species shown in Figure 2 are all controversial because of the scarcity of fossil evidence. Moving from left to right, we see that hominids separated from apes about 5 to 6 million years ago. The first 'ape-man' was *Australopithecus*. Several species have been found in Africa, but, though still disputed, they are generally not thought to be a species of human. They managed to survive for about 3 million years, dying out about 2 million years ago. The first clear evidence for **bipedalism** (walking on two feet) was found in one of its fossils dating back some 3.6 million years.

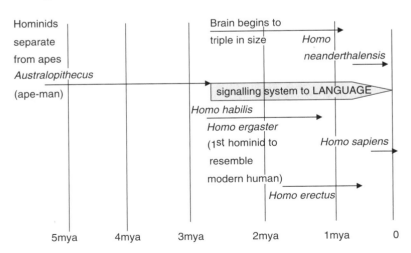

Figure 2 Time frame of changes (*M*illions of *y*ears *a*go abbreviated above as 'mya')

The fossil record then reveals a species of hominid, *Homo habilis* ('handyman') at around 2.3 million years ago. This is the earliest species assigned to the human genus. It made stone tools that unlocked the rich source of calories in meat, a fact that may have helped it survive for as long as 2 million years. Its brain volume was 600–800 cc.

But it is not until 1.8 million years ago that there is a hominid that actually resembles modern man, *Homo ergaster* (early African *Homo erectus* 'upright man'). Aiello believes the latter were the first species of the genus *Homo* to be a dedicated bipedal with the modern vocal apparatus and a lower larynx. As such, it possessed the potential for the range of sounds needed for a complex vocal communication-system. However, its brain was still relatively small, about 800–1,200 cc.

The first evidence of human life found in Europe is *Homo ante-cessor* (similar to *Homo erectus*) about 800,000 years ago. Then later *Homo heidelbergensis* and *Homo neanderthalensis* (Neander-thal) appear from about 600,000 years ago. The latter were hunter-gatherers who lived during the Ice Age. Although they had bigger brains, recent studies show Neanderthal's DNA to be so different from ours that it is not believed to be our most recent common ancestor. Our most recent ancestors were archaic *Homo sapiens* who appeared about 260,000 years ago in Africa. A definite date is 160,000 years ago. By 60,000 years ago they had reached China and by 40,000 years ago Europe. Early *Homo sapiens* had an average brain size of 1,400 cc. while that of modern *Homo sapiens* was slightly larger at 1,500 cc.

Were the Changes Sudden or Gradual?

The traditional view is that evolutionary change is slow, gradual and continuous. But it is also acknowledged that where popula-tions are isolated, the creation of new species can occur rapidly – in as little as hundreds or thousands of years (Gould 1980: 179–185).

However, under normal circumstances, nature does not proceed by leaps and bounds, but at a steady pace. This suggests that language may have developed in a similarly slow and gradual fashion.

How Does Natural Selection Work?

The general impetus for adaptation in any species derives from changes to its environment. These uncontrollable events trigger natural selection processes that are the means by which a species succeeds, or fails, to adapt through reproduction to the challenges of environmental change. These changes may be anatomical or behavioural. It is thought that behaviour which has a survival value can be selected and, over a period of time that is impossible to quantify, become encoded in the genetic script that we call DNA. Once etched in DNA, it modifies the species. When a species finds a niche within a stable environment, it is believed that the rate of evolutionary change slows, or becomes negligible.

The adaptations of the various species of the genus *Homo* shown in Figure 2 were probably caused by the struggle to survive in the face of environmental changes – especially, the onset of several Ice Ages. This challenge would have spurred the development of social skills. But the specific reason for the anatomical changes was the change to a meat-eating diet.

The Same Vocal Tract But Still No Language?

Fossil records show that the modern vocal tract was present *before* modern humans evolved. Does this mean that language or some simple form of language was present before archaic *Homo sapiens* and as early as late *Homo erectus*? The general view is that hominids almost certainly had a signalling system that was more complex than other primates, but that the required intelligence for the neurological coordination of the sounds into a sophisticated communication-system was lacking. A notable exception to this view is held by the distinguished psycholinguist Steven Pinker. He believes that language was present before the taming of fire. How is it possible to determine when language evolved? It is argued the best indicators are

(a) the threefold expansion of the human brain;
(b) artefacts that bear witness to the level of technology;
(c) the presence of symbolism and
(d) more complex social grouping.

Each of these factors will be considered in turn before giving the date that most agree as the likely starting point for a fully developed vocal communication-system that warranted the description language.

The Brain Starts Getting Bigger

At the top of Figure 2, we see that from about 2 million years ago the brain began to expand and grew to three times its original size. Aiello believes that this growth was not uniformly gradual, but that there was rapid expansion from 500,000 years ago and that this event began about 1 million years after the first appearance of *Homo ergaster* who was the first species to possess the modern vocal tract (1998: 31).

In *History of the vertebrate brain*, Gould plays down the significance attributed by so many to this increase in brain size. He does this by placing the increase in perspective. Humans were not the only species whose brain was getting bigger: the same was happening to the brains of all carnivorous mammals, and primates were in the vanguard of this development. While he does concede that the enlargement in the case of humans was not entirely related to body size, as is usually the case, he prefers to emphasize a consequence – the slowing up of infant development (1977: 185).

Mothers now had to give birth to their babies before their heads became too large. As a result, human babies are born helpless, their heads only a quarter of their total size. To hammer home his point, Gould writes that we are born as 'embryos' and remain so for the first nine months of our life. But the positive adaptive feature of this retarded development lay in how it would affect our social evolution. Gould argues that the time spent rearing infants would lead to such a close and intimate bond between mother and child that we became the 'learning animal' (1977: 68) and that this hugely influenced our social evolution. Gould's argument warns us against treating facts – such as brain enlargement – in isolation. Nothing in nature is ever so simple.

Michio Kaku, the internationally acclaimed physicist, describes the human brain 'as a museum preserving its own evolutionary history' (1998: 78–79). This is because it has several distinct concentric layers that show the stages of its history. The deepest and most primitive is the neural chassis that controls basic life functions. This is what fish have. On top and around this is the R-complex that controls aggressive behaviour, territoriality and social hierarchies. Reptiles have both these layers. The next layer is the limbic system that is found in mammals: it controls emotions, social behaviour, smells, memories and so on. Lastly, there is the cortex that surrounds all the previous layers. This controls reason, language and spatial perception among other functions. Figure 3 illustrates this growth and development.

It is believed that language developed its complexity in step with the final 500,000 years of the brain's development. Why did a million years have to pass after *Homo ergaster* before language emerged? Presumably, humankind was not presented with the kind of challenges that prompted the brain's selection for development until the Ice Ages. Only then, in response to the threat to survival, was the success that mental activity endows selected. Those resourceful individuals who were able to make tools, plan out strategies, co-operate with one another – the 'communicators' – would have

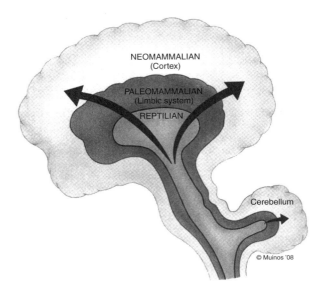

Figure 3 The trajectory of evolution
Source: Illustrations by Hilda R. Muinos from THE USER'S GUIDE TO THE BRAIN by John Ratey, M.D., copyright © 2001 by John J. Ratey, M.D. Used by permission of Pantheon Books, a division of Random House, Inc.

tended to survive and reproduce more. This would have increased their genes while those of the weak dwindled. Their offspring would have learnt their ways by copying their behaviour, and so set in motion a process that would create a mutant gene for an enlarged brain with the memory capacity required for a symbolic system of communication.

However not everyone believes the brain was selected for enlargement to enable a better communication-system. Some argue that language – defined as a cognitive modelling device – might have been built by natural selection, but not necessarily for communication. Gould expresses this alternative view as, 'Our large brains may have originated 'for' some set of necessary skills in gathering food, socializing or whatever; but these skills do not exhaust the limits of what such a complex machine can do' (1980: 57). In other words, speech may have come later, developing out of advanced cognitive abilities. This is what Gould terms a derivative 'exaptation' of an earlier adaptation. Natural selection may build an organ, such as the brain, 'for' a specific function, or a group of functions, but the 'purpose' need not fully specify its capacity. The reason for the quotation marks around 'for' is because biologists do not attribute purpose to the workings of nature. Unlike Gould, orthodox Darwinists maintain that every adaptation is one sort of exaptation. To sum up: the idea that speech developed in tandem with other cognitive abilities is not controversial, to say that it developed out of them later is more controversial, and to call mute modelling capabilities 'language', as Sebeok does (1994: 124/5), is stretching it.

Tool-Making

It is thought that when early hominids left the forest for a habitat of trees bordering on fresh-water lakes, rivers and estuaries, they freed their thumbs and other digits from their original use of grasping the branches of trees in the manner of other primates. Now that these digits were free to fiddle, it is conjectured that some enterprising individual may have used a sharp stone to prise raw meat off bones. Once this practice established itself, it led to the use of stone as a tool. Gradually, the use of these tools became more and more sophisticated and set a precedent for the use of other more specialized artefacts.

In *Darwin's Dangerous Idea*, the American philosopher Daniel Dennett (b. 1942) writes that not only does it require intelligence to make, use and maintain a tool, but that tools also confer potential intelligence on their users because their design amounts to information that could prompt better design (1995: 377). In other words, tools spur the development of visual representation in the mind and, by doing so, promote thinking. Others go even further: they claim that language developed out of this general ability (Ratey 2002: 259). They base their views on recent studies that show the regions of the brain that control the sequenced hand movements used in tool-making are the same as those used for the movements of speech.

Writing on the tool-making traditions of early humans, anthropologist Chris Knight sees three broad stages – the tool tradition of *Homo erectus*, followed by that of *Homo neanderthalensis* (Neanderthals) and, lastly, that of *Homo sapiens* (modern humans). The Acheulian tool tradition of *Homo erectus* lasted a very long time and, Knight claims, it did not exhibit enough diversity or innovation to warrant any claim to culture. He concludes that *Homo erectus* was near primate in behaviour:

> It was to be two million years after the first stone tools and perhaps a million or more from the harnessing of fire before the evolution of technology, physiology and brains would eventually create the material conditions for a breakthrough to symbolic culture. (1991: 258)

Neither did the appearance of modern humans in the Near East and North Africa about 100,000 years ago herald the immediate appearance of more advanced tools. They lived without a fully developed symbolic culture for the first 60,000 years alongside Neanderthals. But when the new and much more diversified artefacts of the Cro-Magnon people established itself approximately 40,000 years ago in Europe, Knight assures us that it exhibited all the hallmarks of symbolic culture-bearing humans and left little doubt that language must have been present. This transition from 60 to 40,000 years ago took place midway during the last glacial period.

Symbolism

While it is clear from the fossil records that early humans possessed the vocal tract for speech, the earliest conclusive evidence for the presence of a fully developed language exists only in the Upper Paleolithic Period (about 40,000 to 35,000 years ago). It was a time when two distinct species of human – Neanderthal and modern humans – co-existed. A period heralded as the time of 'the human revolution' (Mellars 1998: 91–92), or the 'Great Leap Forward' (Diamond 1999: 41). This is because symbolism was found in cave art, on ornaments and on a variety of tools at a number of different locations – Africa, Europe and Australia.

The crucial importance of symbolism to language will be explored later, but if, as many believe, the first step towards language is to break the episodic nature of animal cognition – the way they always seem to be locked into the present – then the cave art of this period bears witness to the fact that the people of that time could think off-line. In other words, they were able to reflect upon past events, think about tomorrow, and so free themselves from the entrapment of the present. The high standard and sequential nature of their paintings of animals and hunting proves this, and scholars are in agreement that language must have been present in a developed form among the Cro-Magnon people.

Social Organization

Humans are fundamentally social animals. This is partly because we are born helpless and have to be reared and cared for. By the time this process is over, individuals have become members of the group and accept this as the norm. Instinctively, early humans would have felt safer and at an advantage as a group facing the daily struggle of existence. Members of the group would probably only leave if they were driven out for some offence, or if they saw some advantage in joining a different group or setting up another. For the majority, life outside the group would have been unthinkable. Being a member of a group, however, involves obligations. As we began to form communities and create larger social environments, individual members would have had to accept obligations, such as work tasks. Put simply, they had to conform to certain rules, and one way they managed to achieve this was by forging a communication-system to make their actions more intelligible.

With the use of tools, hominids began to interact with their environment in a radically different way to other life forms. We began to shape the environment to meet our needs by working together to construct dwellings, set traps and hunt together. Some of these activities could only be done as a group – the rearing and protection of children, the construction of dwellings, hunting, early attempts at growing and tending crops, cooking and sharing food. All of these activities would have involved a degree of social organization which would have stimulated the need for a more efficient means of communication. To avoid argument and confusion, we would have needed to find ways of warning each other of danger, sharing knowledge and desires and setting up rules for peaceful coexistence.

The manufacture of tools during the Middle to Upper Paleolithic Period and the fact that humans were beginning to travel and inhabit most of the continents are a clear indication that social groupings were becoming larger and more complex. The fossil records also show that early humans were living longer. It is believed this was due to better nourishment and better living conditions, such as cave dwelling and man-made shelters. The ability to recreate fire and the uses to which it was put – cooking, making tools, keeping dangerous animals at bay and simply keeping warm – would also have helped lower infant mortality rates and boosted the population.

Yet, despite all this evidence of growing social organization, some still believe that the single most important change that led to greater social intelligence and organization was the change to a meat diet. It meant that children would do less foraging, and this, in turn, would increase **maternal investment** (the time spent by mothers rearing their young) which would make fundamental changes to interpersonal relationships.

A Mimetic Culture

The combined effect of these four developments – brain enlargement, tool making, symbolism and social complexification – was that a 'mimetic culture' gradually emerged. The distinctive feature of such a culture is to represent situations and reflect on them. This can be done individually, such as figuring out how to make a tool, or as a group involved in cooperative endeavours such as performing rituals. Elaborate burials, shrines and art objects all show that ritual began to play a central role in people's lives. Ritual confers symbolic significance upon social acts, often through the dramatic effects of incantation and dance. It is believed that once the re-enactment of events was established as a behavioural pattern, it began to supersede our hitherto unthinking instinctive responses. It helped us to express blindly felt urges. In short, representative acts, especially those that involved language, began to drag our feelings out into the open. Once revealed, they became clearer and more understandable to us. This delineation of emotions would eventually provide a foothold for reasoning to further loosen the bonds of instinct to stimuli. It is as if a sense of our identity began to emerge from the use of language and other forms of expression.

Figure 4 illustrates Donald's idea how in a 'mimetic culture' the whole body was used to re-enact events through rhythm, dance, gesture and sound (Donald qtd. in Aiello 1998: 27).

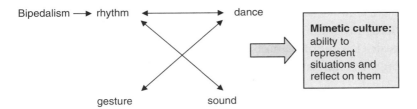

Figure 4 Cross-modality

Did Language Develop from an Earlier Simple Language?

It is assumed that *Homo erectus* and even *Homo habilis* must have had a communication-system more complex than any of today's living primates, but that a more sophisticated communication-system did not occur until, at most, 100,000 years ago, a time when *Neanderthals* and archaic *Homo sapiens* existed side by side.

It is argued by some that Neanderthals had a **protolanguage**, a kind of simple, child-like language that did not develop into the fully developed language of the modern human descendants of *Homo sapiens*. The evidence for this view is that the simpler tools of Neanderthal people reflect a more limited vocabulary and less categorical forms of mental conceptualization. This view is controversial, since the extent we can generalize from tools to the presence of language is disputed.

However, an alternative view, based on the fact that Neanderthal populations lived alongside modern human populations in the Near East and Europe for a very long time, is that Neanderthals did have the capacity for symbolic culture, but that it never became fully realized (Marshack qtd. in Knight 1991: 269). The reason why their alleged equal capacity for symbolic culture did not take off may be accounted for by a controversial theory proposed by zoologist Richard Dawkins. In *The Selfish Gene*, Dawkins proposed a theory that has a direct bearing on claims that language is a genetically programmed component of our behaviour as opposed to a basic element of cultural inheritance. It argues that genes are not the only copiers.

Genes AND Memes!

In a discussion of what there might be in common between life's origins and the emergence of culture, Dawkins argues that the 'genetic takeover' accomplished at life's birth was not to be the only one ever to occur:

> As soon as the primeval soup provided conditions in which molecules could make copies of themselves, the replicators themselves took over. For more than three thousand million years, DNA has been the only replicator worth talking about in the world. But it does not necessarily hold these monopoly rights for all time. Whenever conditions arise in which a new kind of replicator *can* make copies of itself, the new replicators *will* tend to take over, and start a new kind of evolution of their own. Once this new evolution begins, it will in no necessary sense be subservient to the old. (1976: 208)

The origin of culture, according to Dawkins, was launched by just such a takeover. He argues that memes took over some or all of the copying from genes. A successful '**meme**' (from the Greek 'mimēsis', meaning 'mimicry') is a portion of cultural tradition – such as an idea – which survives in the memories of successive generations and is capable of evolving at a very rapid pace. Just as genes propagate themselves in the gene pool by leaping from cell to cell, so, too, according to this view, do memes. They do this by a process which, in the broad sense, can be called 'learning' or 'imitation'. In other words, there are genes for replicating biological features and there are memes that replicate aspects of behaviour that have been selected as aiding the species. History or cultural change, in this view, is basically the evolution of memes.

Later, in the face of a storm of protest, Dawkins (1982) argued less for the existence of memes than for a biological perspective that recognized the beaver's dam, the spider's web and the bird's nest as on a par with the beaver's teeth, the spider's legs and the bird's wings. On this point, Dennett is in agreement with Dawkins. This is because Dennett believes there is a tendency for the **genotype** (the information in the genome that gets passed on between generations) to follow the lead of the **phenotype** (the behaviour of the individual organism). Variations in the behaviour of the phenotype, especially advantageous traits of behaviour, give the genotype better chances of survival. Dennett writes, 'In the long run, natural selection – redesign at the genotype level – will tend to *follow the lead of* and *confirm* the directions taken by the individual organisms' successful explorations – redesign at the individual or phenotype level' (1995: 78). The italics are Dennett's and they are there to emphasize the importance of considering an organism at its phenotypic level.

Dawkins's explanation could account for the runaway increase in the population of modern humans and the demise of Neanderthals. If *Homo sapiens* became more skilled in transmitting their culture than Neanderthals, it would have tilted the balance of power in their favour. The fact that Neanderthals had larger brains leaves a lot of questions unanswered, however. Some argue that their brains may have been bigger, but they lacked certain important cerebral connections. This seems more likely since there is still no proof that memes exist. We shall probably never know. But what we can say with certainty is that language would have enabled cultural innovations to be passed on orally to successive generations and that this would have quickened the pace of change because cultural evolution operates much faster than genetic evolution. If *Homo sapiens* were better at this, their technology would have quickly outpaced that of Neanderthals. And, who knows, perhaps we turned our better weapons against the physically stronger, but mentally weaker, until the last surviving alternative human species became extinct.

Summary

We can state that on the basis of

(i)   the presence of the modern vocal tract from about 2 million years ago,

(ii)   the enlargement of the brain,

(iii) the slow development of infants,

(iv)   more complex social grouping from about 400 to 300,000 years ago,

(v)   the modern human genome from at least 200,000 years ago,

(vi)   mimetic cultures from at least 100,000 years ago and

(vii) symbolic sequential art from 45,000 years ago

that language certainly existed at the start of the Middle to Upper Paleolithic Period some 45,000 years ago and that it probably developed for purposes of more efficient social interaction in the face of numerous challenges to our survival.

Given that archaeological evidence of grave offerings from 90 to 100,000 years ago could be construed as a kind of symbolic act and that the earliest known human remains that share the same DNA date from 200,000 years ago, it may be possible to suggest an even earlier date for the emergence of language – perhaps, as early as 200,000 years ago in some simple, or developing, form. In one species of human – *Homo sapiens* – it seems likely that a genetic mutation occurred which allowed a representational system such as language to develop in an already enlarged brain. Once language reached a certain point of development, it enabled the transmission of culture which led to the dominance of one species and the demise of others of the same genus.

Six of One and Half a Dozen of the Other?

So is language genetic after all? Is Chomsky right? And are the 'environmentalists' losing the argument? Having claimed that a Universal Grammar is innately specified in a 'language organ', one would imagine that Chomsky would welcome a Darwinian account of how such an organ could have evolved. Yet he does not. He points out that Darwin may have given natural selection pride of place among evolutionary processes, but he also recognized other processes at work. Some of these were termed non-adaptive because they do not promote an organism's survival. He cites how Darwin showed that adaptive change in one part of an organism could lead to non-adaptive modifications in another part, and that, even in those cases where an organ had developed under the influence of selection for a specific role, there was no reason preventing it developing other roles (Chomsky 2002: 47). In other words, it is such a complicated scenario that he wants to keep his options open on the question of whether language was *specifically* selected. At the moment, he seems to be hoping for a physical explanation of how the language faculty 'may be the result of the functioning of physical and chemical laws for a brain that has reached a certain level of complexity' (2002: 57).

However, at our present level of understanding, not even physicists have any clear answers. Michio Kaku believes it is highly unlikely that a language or a 'grammar gene' could ever be isolated. Language is most likely connected to other cognitive faculties and, if it is genetic, it is almost bound to be polygenic. Polygenic traits usually involve interactions with several other genes *as well as* the environment (1998: 227–228). This reflects the complex relationship between genotype and phenotype and explains why identical twins raised in different environments can differ. But there is a further complication: genes can have multiple functions. This means they can be involved in different tasks – language and, for example, movement. Add to this the fact that some only come into play after birth to switch others on and off and you have an extremely complex arrangement. To discover the structure and properties of these complex proteins is going to take many years.

As far as the evolution of language is concerned, there is not enough hard evidence for either side – the biological or socio-cultural – to claim outright victory. At present, evidence from other quarters seems to be favouring the biological, but the jury is still out and will probably be out for a very long time before a clear judgement resolves this question once and for all. In the meantime, it remains a fascinating debate.

Chapter 1: When early hominids changed to a meat diet it prompted anatomical changes that would eventually provide a vocal apparatus that could make the wider variety of sounds required for an advanced signalling system. However, millions of years would pass before a mutation would cause one species of humans, our ancestors, to use an already enlarged brain to develop a communication-system that offered an evolutionary advantage in terms of more efficient social organization and cultural evolution. The key characteristic of this communication-system was its symbolic nature.

Study Questions

1. There are other theories of language origin. One is called the 'onomatopoeic', another 'interjective' and a third 'synergastic'. Find out what you can about them, and any others, and discuss your findings.
2. Do you think language emerged as an accidental offshoot of early humankind's ability to visualize tools? Or, do you think it was selected in much the same way as arms and legs are? Or do you think living in a group the most important factor? Jot down your views on these rival explanations.
3. Find out what these words mean – glossogenetic, semiogenetic. Explain the difference between them.
4. Do you think language developed so slowly that it was unnoticed? Or do you think someone at some point must have realized that a new way of representing reality had been stumbled upon?

Chapter 2: In the next chapter, we shall consider the connection between language and consciousness.

Is Language Exclusive to Humans?

The Big Difference is Consciousness

The answer to this chapter's question is a resounding, Yes! Has your dog or cat ever invited you to its birthday party? No? Well, I'm sure you won't be surprised to hear that it's because of a quantum difference in consciousness. Our consciousness enables us to communicate symbolically, a fact that qualifies for the description language. Animals do not possess such a system. For many, this creates a chasm between us. They argue it represents a discontinuity, one so great that it leaves us biologically isolated. They cite the restricted repertoire of animal communications – most of it is about sex, survival, identity of caller, territorial rights, etc. – and then return to extol the virtues of our wonderfully complex brains.

Unfortunately, this praise overlooks the fact that language could not have suddenly appeared, that it must have cranked itself out of something, and that that something must have been whatever cognitive capabilities we had prior to its development. It is this that we once shared with other primates and its development that was crucial to our gradual and then more accelerated divergence. Does anything remain of those links we once shared over 5 million years ago with other primates?

In this chapter, we shall begin by showing where our manner of communicating is closest to animals. We shall then go on to describe different kinds of human symbolic behaviour. This will lead into a general description of human consciousness which shows how some of its key characteristics affect language. Next, the question of whether language has a specific location in the brain will be considered and, latterly, how we need to be wary of our descriptions of complicated and little understood phenomena.

Where the Links Still Lie

Animal communication studies are in their infancy. So before we can begin, we have to be aware of just how much we don't know and, possibly, may never know. According to Peter Marler of the Center for Animal Behavior of the University of California, we know nothing about the electrical communication of fish, chemical signals of insects, the substrate vibrations of frogs and insects, the ultrasonic signals of bats and rodents, or the infrasound of elephants (Jablonski & Aiello 1998: 1). The commonest medium used by animals to know something is smell, but precisely what an animal can tell from smells is largely unknown. Against this background, it is hardly surprising that **ethologists** (those who study animal behaviour) confine their investigations to what can be observed. In the case of researchers interested in signalling systems, this usually means matching certain behaviour to specific sounds.

At our present level of knowledge regarding this narrow spectrum of animal behaviour three kinds of vocal signals have been observed. The first are **affective**, or emotional, signals. These belong to all mammals, humans included. They are not considered symbolic because they do not stand for anything other than the emotion being portrayed. This kind of communication is called **iconic** (because the sound is thought to resemble the emotion) and described as **reflexive** (lacking intention or voluntary control). A howl of pain is an expression of pain. There appears to be no cognitive content to such messages, they are purely emotional.

The second kind of signal is more specific than the first and is considered symbolic. Certain animals use different calls to alert others to different situations. Most studied among these animals are vervet monkeys. These monkeys have different alarm calls for different predators – one for eagles, another for leopards, another for snakes, etc. Ethologists remain neutral on what's going on in their heads when they make these calls. For example, whether there is an image of a particular predator, or whether the call is a cue for a certain action, such as go 'down a hole' or 'up a tree'. For this reason, they describe these signals as having a functional, rather than a fully symbolic, reference.

The third kind of signal is learnt, passed down from parent to young. For example, songbirds learn songs, but they recombine what they have learnt from their parents in many new and different sequences and so develop a large sign repertoire. This is creative. However, it is believed the sequences are emotional and bear no meaning. Interestingly, it is thought that the impetus for this creativity does not derive from any direct external stimulus, but from within. It is conjectured that the animals – whales included – want to create diversity for its own sake, to amuse themselves, alleviate boredom or loneliness.

From this brief account, we can see that the likeliest link between us and the way certain animals communicate will lie in our emotional, nonverbal behaviour. The study of nonverbal behaviour is divided between **kinesics** (study of relationship between body motions, blushes, shrugs, eye movement, facial expression, etc.) and **paralanguage** (the study of optional vocal effects, tone of voice, etc.). These actions and sounds comprise our iconic or nonverbal codes. Linguists are not very interested in this aspect of communication because it does not involve language. Some also deride it as primitive because the signals are vague. For example, a person might grunt, but what does this grunt mean? Is it a grunt of pain, tiredness, satisfaction? Even context may not help to clarify its meaning. Some linguists believe language has replaced these 'cruder' systems.

Communication theorist Gregory Bateson argues against this view (2000: 418). He believes they were not replaced, but became more complex, some even developing into art forms such as music, dance, poetry, etc. He believes that they could not be replaced because not only do they add the feeling and emotion that is so crucial to relationships, but they also help us detect the honesty or insincerity of a message. When a salesman is smiling and assuring you it's the last model they have and the next customer is going to snap it up, subconsciously you are probably listening to his tone and observing his actions more than his words. Is he trying to con you? The clues to sincerity will not necessarily be in his words, but in the actions and overtones of feeling that suffuse them.

Now that we have established at least one link between the way we and certain animals communicate, let's consider the nature of our symbolic behaviour and ask if, as is so often the case, it should be portrayed as so utterly rational and different to that of animals.

Kinds of Symbolic Action

The English philosopher Alfred North Whitehead (1861–1947) is best known for his collaboration with Bertrand Russell on a colossal work entitled *Principia Mathematica*. Less well known is that later in life he became interested in the function of symbols in society, an interest that eventually led him to develop a philosophy called 'process philosophy', although he preferred to call it 'philosophy of the organism'. He gave a series of lectures at the University of Virginia which formed the basis for a slim book entitled *Symbolism* (1927). Its aim was to show the influence of symbolism on human life.

He begins by distinguishing three kinds of symbolic action: instinctive, reflex and conditioned. The first is the most primitive and totally analysable in terms of the environmental conditions that cause it in the first instance. Here, environment refers to both physical and social surroundings. Instinctive action is immediate adjustment to immediate environmental conditions. For example, a room becomes crowded, you feel hot and uncomfortable, you do something – loosen a garment, open a window, whatever. These actions are closely related to bodily states. Others concern basic instincts such as fear, joy, disgust, etc. that can be aroused by sights and sounds. For example, you see the carcass of a dead dog, you grimace. Or you see a round-eyed, chubby-cheeked baby and you can't help exclaiming, 'Ooh!'

Reflex action is half way between instinct and conditioned action. It is totally dependent on sense-presentation. This is because it is hindered by thought. Whitehead puts it like this, 'The response of action to symbol may be so direct as to cut out any effective reference to the ultimate thing symbolized' (1927: 73). This is the kind of action soldiers are trained to achieve: to obey orders immediately without questioning. In this scenario, thought is the enemy of action.

The third kind of symbolic behaviour is conditioned action. This is shaped by habit. Repetition makes this kind of behaviour so familiar that most of the time it escapes our notice. As conventions emerge from the regularity of certain common actions, the role of thought decreases because the known no longer requires any further attention. So, for example, when we hear mother call, 'Kettle's boiling!' this is meant to elicit action not a contemplation of water changing to steam. This is the kind of symbolic action that is most familiar to us and which probably comprises much of what we say, hear and do on an everyday basis.

Are all the symbolic actions of language like these? Of course not. Whitehead's analysis is far from exhaustive: it was a beginning that predates the much more detailed work of J. L. Austin, Paul Grice and John Searle in the sixties on speech act theory of which more will be said in a later chapter. One obvious omission is that a good deal of language is used for socializing. This kind of talk is not about getting somebody to do something, but about maintaining social relations. Also, there are occasions when the actions urged by the symbols of speech may not be familiar and a person has to consciously 'think' about what s/he is supposed or expected to do. It is only in these situations that we can properly think of language as requiring thought. Most of the time, speaking is simply unreflective social activity.

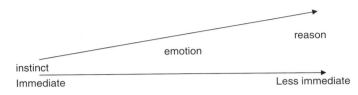

Figure 5 From instinct to emotion to reason

The differences between these types of symbolic action are often explained in terms of immediacy. It is argued that those caused by fear or joy would be as direct and instinctive as an animal's, while others requiring thought would be at the other end of the scale. In a later chapter, we will question this notion of immediacy, but for the moment we illustrate the movement away from immediacy through the agency of language towards thought as in Figure 5.

In Figure 5, the links to animal communication stop at the threshold of emotion. All animals can express emotional states, although the gradations along that continuum will not be the same as ours for the simple reason that language feeds back into emotion creating ever subtler shades. Here are a few examples to illustrate this scale.

'Ow!' [Pain]

'Attention! Quick march!' [Drill sergeant's order]

'I love you.' [Emotional]

'I'm going to bed.' [Conditioned]

'I like your new shoes.' [Social]

'Do you think you should speak to him first about this?' [Situation requiring thought]

'The quantity of information is usually expressed as the log to base 2 of the improbability of the actual event.' [Reasoning]

When language's links to thought become the sole focus of attention and no consideration is given to instincts, feelings, emotions and imagination it is bound to make the differences between us and animals seem unbridgeable. The extent to which some actions are instinctive, reflexive and conditioned is where our behaviour overlaps with that of certain animals. The fact that our symbolic behaviour is often less than rational suggests that there may be more continuity between us than many would like to admit. But there is no shame in this: if habits blinker us, it is to give us a blessed relief from thought and hasten action. It is an economy in the cause of action.

The reader should be alerted to the fact that for most **generative linguists** (those who support generative grammar, especially of the Chomskyan variety) any talk of stimulus and conditioned response is an anathema. They prefer to talk of language behaviour as creative and free from any connection to stimuli. They stress the expressive variation of language, its open-endedness, and how responses are not determined by stimulus. For example, Ray Jackendoff writes, 'Aside from stereotyped utterances like "Hi, how are you?" and "Please pass the salt," most of the sentences we speak in the course of the day are sentences we have never heard or spoken in their entirety before' (1994: 11). It is this alleged newness that they believe warrants the description 'creative'. But others do recognize that the use of 'creative' in this context is unconventional and place guarded quotes around it (e.g. Belletti & Rizzi in Chomsky 2002: 2).

While creativity is certainly an attribute of the system of language, does it necessarily follow from this that we can describe talking as creative? Creative acts usually involve effort: Picasso famously characterized his work as requiring 1 per cent inspiration and 99 per cent hard work. Spoken language requires no effort and serves a practical, rather than a creative, purpose. Nevertheless, this view is now common in linguistics. I leave the reader to decide just how much we say in an average day is 'stereotyped' or 'new', and if we can call that 'newness' creative.

Now that we have begun to put the role of thinking in its narrower sense of reasoning into perspective, let us turn our attention to its broader sense which we will characterize as the silent mode of language.

The Silent Mode of Language

The silent mode of language, sometimes called self-talk, is often loosely referred to as 'thinking'. This broad definition of 'thinking' does not refer to reasoning or the solving of problems, but to talking to yourself, a kind of internal running commentary on what is going on both around and inside you. Is this activity different to speech? Or is it the same only unvoiced? There is a traditional and a more subtle modern opinion that argue they are different. Let's consider the traditional first and the modern one later.

In the past, some linguists argued that inner speech was inferior to its spoken mode because it was fragmentary, replete with ellipses, and lacked proper grammatical connections (e.g. Jakobson 1990: 98–99). But surely the grammar, vocabulary and sound in our mental 'ear' must be roughly the same. If it were not, meaning would be lost. The rules of grammar could be bent a little, but they would have to be in rough agreement with spoken language because it is its image and there is nothing else for it to model itself upon. And, as to whether inner speech is inferior, if both convey meaning then they must be functionally equivalent. If we searched for similarities instead of differences, the most obvious would be that our self-talk takes the form of a dialogue. We create the illusion of another, a twin or double self to which we direct our silent chatter.

If the only difference between external and internal speech is that one is voiced and the other not, then the connection between thought, language and action is unbroken. Thought (internal speech) is not separate from conduct, but continuous with it. Thought is part of the activity of humans, sometimes prompting real action and, at other times, imagined or anticipated actions. Speech reports on the activity of thinking.

Drawing from linguist Derek Bickerton's influential book *Language and Human Behaviour*, let's now turn our attention to consciousness, the dwelling place of language.

Consciousness-1

Every living organism is to a greater or lesser extent aware of its environment and itself in relation to its environment. Bickerton calls this awareness of the environment consciousness-1 (1995: 127). From tiny amoeba-sized creatures up to insects up to animals and humans, sensory input reacts upon the nervous system of the brain to create this mind-state.

The organism reacts to input by trying to maintain **homeostasis** – a state that favours continued existence. It is from this *having to do* certain things, usually because of patterns and regularities in the environment, that habits spring. Thus, if sunlight turned to shade and the temperature dropped, a creature that preferred a higher temperature to feel comfortable (and ultimately to survive) would seek a warmer spot. Controversy exists as to whether the stimulus derives solely from the environment or exhibits a purpose on the part of the organism or a combination of both.

The differences between species with regard to consciousness-1 vary in much the same way as intelligence does. Thus, it is customary to think of a dog as more intelligent than a mouse, or a snake, or a fly, because its sensory capacity, as well as the variety of responses it shows, appear more advanced than that of mice, reptiles and insects. This is because other aspects of brain function, for example, memory, attention mechanisms, etc., interact with consciousness-1 to add greater breadth and depth in some species than in others.

Consciousness-2

Consciousness-1 is not only conscious of things in the environment – for example, changes in light intensity, the appearance of potential predators or mates, of homeostasis-threatening experiences (e.g. pain) or homeostasis-enhancing experiences (e.g. pleasure) – it also offers feedback that creates a limited consciousness of self. For example, the claws of a crab could not converge on a moving shrimp if the crab's brain had no information about the movement of its own claws. At best, this basic kind of feedback is only considered to be an on-line (moment by moment) consciousness of self and does not constitute knowledge or awareness of self.

The boundary that marks the main difference between the consciousness-1 of all other life forms and human consciousness is the distinction between on- and off-line processing. Unlike animals, humans have the ability to process off-line. This means we can review present perceptions in terms of the past and even project them in terms of the future. In short, humans are 'conscious of being conscious'. Bickerton calls this additional consciousness, consciousness-2 (1995: 58).

Consciousness-2 provides us with awareness of consciousness-1. We not only see a cloud, we are aware that we see a cloud. Consciousness-1 is wholly absorbed in mediation – the nervous system of the brain making sense of what is going on outside and reacting accordingly. There is nothing in consciousness-1 that could make it aware of itself or the world it is mediating. For consciousness of consciousness-1 to arise there would have to be some part of the brain that is detached from the constant traffic of information between brain and environment. That detached area is consciousness-2.

It is generally agreed that only the emergence of language could have created areas from which the workings of animal

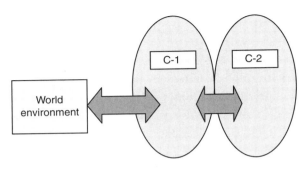

Figure 6 Human consciousness

consciousness could be objectively perceived. However, as explained in Chapter 1, it is also recognized that the ability to represent must have developed up to a certain point before the breakthrough into language or in tandem with language. Whichever was the case, the rapid expansion of the brain must have been crucial to its development.

Figure 6 summarizes what has been said about language and the nature of human consciousness.

The figure shows that only consciousness-1 (C-1) is directly linked to the reality outside us. The double-headed arrow indicates that there is feedback between the environment and the organism. On its own, this would comprise animal consciousness – a serial processing of incoming sensory data resulting in appropriate reactions that are directed towards maintaining homeostasis. This is essentially an on-line process. Humans have this ability, but in addition, due to the emergence of language, we also have consciousness-2 (C-2). Consciousness-2 is not directly linked to the environment, but reaches it through consciousness-1. Because of its detachment and possession of a representational system, it is conscious of consciousness-1 and has the ability to process off-line. This dual arrangement of the human brain has been described by researchers in artificial intelligence as resembling a parallel computer (consciousness-2) hooked up to a serial computer (consciousness-1).

The hallmark of our kind of consciousness is, then, this being conscious of our consciousness. This is often viewed as a breach with nature, but it could also be viewed as being more in the world. Whereas animals seem to be locked into what they are feeling in the here-and-now, we can detach ourselves from the demands of the present. What enables this is not just the presence of language, but a capacity for remembering. Memory tempers our present.

This form of consciousness enables us to be as aware of the images in our heads as we are of the reality outside – a dualism often expressed as 'self and other' or 'image and object'. Although this double-take on reality does not operate simultaneously but requires a shift of attention, it has created a relation of knowing that begs the question which is truer – the sensations in the mind or the sense data that cause them. Over the ages, philosophers have argued for one or the other and, in the process, a thousand other dichotomies have been spawned – mind-nature, mental-physical, knowledge-experience, thought-language, subjective-objective, etc. Some, though fewer, have argued that the relation between them is most important. We shall return to this thorny question later, but for the moment let's look at the kind of language housed within this unique form of consciousness.

The Nature of Language

On the basis of this description of human consciousness, we are now in a position to list five general, universal properties of language. The first two concern sound, the third the mental operation of joining sound to meaning to produce the linguistic sign, the fourth the ordering of those signs and the last time.

1. One Sound at a Time

Language is a **serial**, one-sound-at-a-time process. This is not merely because we have only one vocal tract: it is because our consciousness, and particularly our brain's attention mechanisms, normally only deal with one thing at a time. While hundreds of things are monitored and can be upgraded at any moment, the attention must be undivided. Consciousness-2 does not change the attention mechanism, but increases its range to include mental states so that it is not only concerned with what is happening out there, but also reacting to internal states. Hence, the nature of language corresponds to the serial nature of consciousness-1's processing – it is a one-sound-at-a-time process that makes language both serial and **linear** (string-like). Despite sounds only coming one at a time, humans can produce 12 speech sounds per second and we can understand our mother tongue even when it is sped up to 50 speech sounds per second (Winston et al. 2004: 169).

2. Contrasting Sounds

Individual units of sound are called phonemes and, although they may have no meaning in themselves, they exhibit a **feature of contrast** (also described as **phonological opposition**). For example, all consonants obstruct the flow of air from the lungs. Some stop it briefly, for example [p, t, k, b], while others block it more forcibly, for example [f, s, v, z]. Naturally, these contrasts depend upon the ability of listeners to distinguish them. The fact that they can means that we can describe the contrasts as psychologically real. Although the sounds of phonemes vary slightly from speaker to speaker, the ability of people to still recognize them proves the existence of a boundary between one and another. This is termed **discreteness**. Its opposite is **continuity**, or **continuous variation**, or **gradience**. Thus, 'bit', 'but', 'bet', 'bat' are only differentiated by single vowel phonemes. If the intensity or gradience of 'bit' were increased to 'b-i-i-i-t', it would make no sense to a listener. If some intermediate vowel sound were made in voicing these words, it would either not be recognized or construed as a mispronunciation or an unknown word.

3 a. Joining Sound to Meaning

The relevance of boundaries to phonemes lies not only within the system of sound contrasts, but also in their connection to meaning via a postulated higher level of **morphemes** (the discrete elements of meaning, e.g. the {un-} and {do} of 'undo'). This is because it is the differentiation of meaning that gives phonemes their relevance. **Duality of patterning** (or **double articulation**) refers to the property of language to have two levels of structure that can combine. It is generally accepted that all communication-systems have at least one level of primary units. The presence of this design feature in animal communication is a matter of degree. In human systems, it is conjectured that there is a first level of articulation where a message is structured into meaningful units. These are morphemes, the building blocks of words. At the second level of articulation, there are phonemes. Each level has its own principles of organization, but the function of phonemes is to differentiate the meaning of morphemes. The main difference between our use of this feature and that of animals is the sheer scale of our combination of minimal meaningless phonemes to form new messages. For example, chimpanzees use about 30 to 36 sounds, not a meagre amount, but they do not combine them in a meaningful manner.

The actual operation of how we attach sound to meaning is accomplished at such astonishing speed that it is probably best to conceive of it as one act and to view these descriptions of matching the elements of one 'level of structure' to another as convenient abstractions for the purpose of explanation. Sound and meaning must already be linked and only await excitation to a representative form. Let's now consider the product of this firing of associated elements.

3 b. The Linguistic Sign

When the brain performs, it generates mind and mind, if it so wills, calls forth the signs of language. The sign, by definition, has to mean something. When it is voiced, it becomes a physical **signal** with a mental counterpart. The number of dimensions attributed to the sign depends upon the theoretical model. Most models attribute two or three. The main point is that the sign has at least two faces: its conceptual aspect mirroring the meaning of both the acoustic image and its physical signal. Given the dual nature of our consciousness, it should come as no surprise that its brainchild, the sign, should also exhibit a dualism – sound and meaning.

One of the most influential models of the linguistic sign is Saussure's and for this reason it deserves our attention. Comparing the linguistic sign with the two sides of a sheet of paper Saussure wrote: 'thought is the front and the sound the back; one cannot cut the front without cutting the back at the same time' (1916: 113). He went on to define the linguistic sign as uniting, 'not a thing and a name, but a concept and a sound-image' (1916: 66). The latter was not a physical thing, but a 'psychological imprint of the sound' (1916: 66). He describes the sound-image as sensory, and the concept as more abstract. Clearly, both phenomena are extremely difficult to describe because they are immanent, non-physical and, therefore, unobservable.

Figure 7 represents the two sides of this psychological entity within an ellipse which stands for the sign as a whole. In the ellipse on the right, the Latin word *arbor* is an example of a sequence of sound-images referring to the concept 'tree'. The use of a picture to portray the concept is unfortunate because it looks like a conifer when really it is meant to suggest a prototype that suggests all the

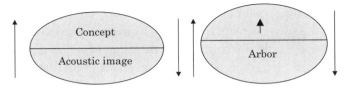

Figure 7 Saussure's model of the linguistic sign (left) and exemplification (right)

possible characteristics of trees. The arrows indicate the psychological association between the two aspects of the sign and refer to the processes of speech production and reception.

Later, Saussure introduced the terms *signifié* (for concept) and *signifiant* (for sound-image). The English translation for these terms are, respectively, **signified** and **signifier**. Traditionally, linguistics only studied the voiced aspect of the signifier. This effectively shut off a useful avenue of enquiry into the nature of language. It may even have closed off one half of the nature of language from linguistic enquiry. The result was that, until the 1960s, research into language's silent, inner mode was conducted by separate disciplines, such as psychology and philosophy of mind.

Saussure, answering objections to his claim that we cannot think without language, replied that our thoughts can only dispense with words by using a different set of signs, such as the notations used for music or mathematics. While his response highlighted the importance of symbolic signs as the atom of all representational systems – whether for language, mathematics or music – it did not draw enough attention to the fact that these signs also have to be ordered to become meaningful and that some of them must show how others are linked.

4. Ordering the Signs

The sequential nature of both language's internal sound-images and its external sound signals created the need for some way of indicating the semantic relations between the units of that stream of sound. Enter rules of syntax. If signs were not ordered by rules of syntax, it would not comprise a truly linguistic system: it would be an incomplete representational one. This is Bickerton's main thesis. On first reading, it seems innocent enough, but on the basis of this many proclaim syntax to be the most important aspect of language. Others retort that without symbolism there would be nothing for syntax to work on.

The relation between the rules of syntax that govern acceptable combinations of signs and the signs of the lexicon that are selected and slotted into the patterning are best envisaged as intersecting axes. In Saussure's terminology these axes are termed the **syntagmatic** and **paradigmatic**. If these terms seem cumbersome, just think of 'combination' for the first and 'substitution' for the second. The former describes the relation between words which are simultaneously present. For example, at word level, the morphemes {*un-*} {*know*} and {*-ing*} are syntagmatically related in a particular way in the word *unknowing* and the words 'the' 'strange' 'man' are syntagmatically related in the noun phrase 'the strange man'. Paradigmatic relations describe the relation between a set of linguistic terms which constitute choices, so that only one of them may be present at a time. For example, in the sentence 'they love tv', 'love' could be substituted by 'like', 'dislike', 'hate', 'watch', but not, 'when', etc.

While the rules of syntax are finite but allow for an infinite number of combinations, the paradigmatic rules that govern the choice of words seem to represent pockets of order that are more particular and less susceptible to generalizations. This is partly why language change can occur more easily in the lexicon – their knock-on effect is limited, while grammatical changes can have a domino effect.

The stability of grammar, or what is perceived as its greater resistance to change, is another reason for some to declare it the backbone, core or essence of language. A common analogy is that grammar is the skeleton and lexicon the flesh of language. Linguist

Michael Halliday prefers to use the term 'lexicogrammar' to show that they work together, complementing one another, and that the overriding consideration is not which is more important, but the creation of meaning (2003: 83).

5. Delayed Response

Because language depends on an acoustic medium for its transmission, it creates a response delay. The time it takes the listener to hear and interpret the speaker's message is the measure of that delay. The delay is not entirely due to listener–speaker roles, however. The symbolic nature of the linguistic sign means that it is not the thing itself, but stands for it and thereby requires interpretation. This heuristic act is often cited as the defining feature of rational beings. It is claimed that both the air as a channel and symbolism mediate and that, however instantaneous the act of interpretation may seem, it is different to the direct sensations of touch, taste, smell, sound and sight.

The representative nature of the symbol – the way it substitutes itself for the real and the unreal – underpins our ability to refer to things outside of our immediate sensory field. Technically, this is termed **displacement**. Closely related to this capacity is **stimulus-freedom**. Unlike animals who are described as **stimulus-bound**, we are not compelled to react in the same predictable manner to signs of language that act as stimuli, but free to do as we wish.

In principle, this is true. When someone asks, 'Would you like another cup of tea?' or tells you, 'This is a good novel', your response is not controlled by their words. You could respond in any way you liked. But, in practice, we know that our reactions are tuned to respond in an appropriate manner. When they do not, the only way they can escape criticism is if they are in the cause of humour or comedy. This is because the moment we interact with people a principle of cooperation comes into operation. This question is related to an earlier one – whether we could describe talking as creative. Only this time, it is more complicated because it concerns not just the meaning of the word 'stimulus', but associated words, concepts and theory. We will not be able to resolve all the issues concealed in this stark contrast, but we do need to dispel the illusion of simplicity it creates.

Why has the abstract principle of human freedom from stimulus been selected as more important than the principle of cooperation that generally operates in practice? Quoting La Forge, a commentator on Descartes' work, Chomsky writes that whereas animals are compelled, humans are only incited or inclined by the signs (stimuli) of language (1980: 7). We always have the option of opting out and that is our ultimate freedom. Now this is true, and if we were always bound to react in a predictable manner language would probably not have evolved. But, even though this ultimate freedom exists, it does not change the fact that for the better part of most days we are 'incited and inclined' to follow the stimuli of language. The literary effect of polarizing the extremes – stimulus-free or -bound – makes it appear as if there is no middle ground, when there is. It also suggests that a facile choice has to be made between the two. But the truth is far more complex: our moods, feelings and thoughts are interacting with a host of external stimuli, linguistic and non-linguistic. The language that may or may not arise from that kaleidoscopic play is never entirely free or governed. Sometimes inner states have the upper hand and, other times, external factors take the reins. That's why we need to guard ourselves against this style of thinking that reduces everything to black-and-white choices: it simplifies to the point of falsification.

Summary

Of the five universal properties of language outlined above, at least three seem to mirror the dual aspect of our consciousness. The sound systems of language form contrasts of a binary nature, the linguistic sign has a dual patterning of sound and meaning, and its symbolic nature by standing for, or in place of, creates the need for the encoding and decoding of messages. Only the first and last properties seem non-dualistic. The fact that we can only make one sound at a time has more to do with attention mechanisms and the sensorimotor functions of the body. How we order signs may be genetically encoded or derive from habitual exposure to language or a combination of both. The next question we will consider is whether language has a location in the brain.

Is Language a Module in the Brain?

There are two views on this question, holistic and modular. The holistic view argues that language is part and parcel of our general cognitive abilities and that it is impossible to separate its workings from them. The modular view claims that the brain is made up of separate, specialized modules that control different activities and that language is one or more of these. The latter is central to Chomsky's belief in a language acquisition device.

Neuroscience (the study of the brain) is still in its infancy and there is a huge amount that we do not know about this most complex part of our bodies. As a result, no one on either side of this debate doubts the difficulty of separating the workings of language from our other cognitive activities. It boils down to a difference of degree: how separate is language? Before considering the nature of that difference, let's list some of the things that are known about the brain:

(i) Only human brains have two hemispheres.
(ii) Language is distributed throughout the brain and can vary significantly from one person to the next.
(iii) Nevertheless, most language areas are found clustered around the Sylvian fissure, a long groove in the **cortex** (outer layer) of the left hemisphere.

(iv) The same **neurons** (nerve cells) are used to activate speech and interpretation. So speech production and comprehension are not independent systems, a point that seems to argue against a rigid separation of thought from language.

(v) Some language areas are incredibly specialized, almost comically so. For example, there are specific locations responsible for naming vegetables, another for living things, one for gem stones and another for fabrics. There are even different centres for regular and irregular verbs, though this can vary among people.

(vi) We are not sure how all the different locations are integrated but, despite this, independent systems have been proposed for grammar, meaning and word formation. This is because very specific speech disorders result from damage to particular parts of the brain.

(vii) Independent systems or not, language is not a step-by-step process, but one of parallel activation of many small areas. Even silent thinking will activate the same areas as speech. This point strongly suggests continuity between thought and language.

(viii) Other regions of the brain are also involved with language's operations. For example, there is constant interaction with areas that control movement because gesture and speech involve movement. The emotion that we convey with intonation comes from the right hemisphere.

(ix) The plasticity of the brain allows neural connections to rewire after damage and this provides some hope of recovery from accidents, especially for young people.

(x) The timeline of language development in children is consistent across cultures. The process begins before birth – neural connections are being made as a foetus hears speech in the womb.

(xi) We lose the flexibility to form new language connections by the time we are seven years old. Second languages learnt after that are stored in separate neural systems and these can vary greatly between individuals.

(xii) Language is intricately bound up with our cognition, but not controlled by exactly the same neural connections.

Historically, the view that language is a separate module stems from the pioneering work of brain surgeons such as Paul Broca and Carl Wernicke in language neurology in the latter part of the nineteenth century. In 1864, the Frenchman Paul Broca announced his discovery that damage to a particular area of the brain – now named after him – caused **aphasia** (language disorders due to brain damage) of a very specific kind. Patients spoke very slowly, without rhythm or intonation and, most interestingly, without grammar. The little connectors of grammar – 'if', 'to', 'of', etc. – were gone. Ten years after this discovery, the German Carl Wernicke found a different kind of aphasia due to damage in another part of the brain. His patients spoke very fluently, the rhythm and intonation of their speech was normal, their grammar was intact, but they were speaking nonsense and could not comprehend anything that was said to them.

Gradually, a picture began to emerge of how language might be organized in the brain. Called the standard model, it goes something like this: first, the auditory area just behind the ears receives input from the ears and sends it on to Wernicke's area which is just behind the left ear and in charge of comprehension. Then Wernicke's area sends it on to Broca's area which gives it grammatical form and passes it onto the motor area for speech output. There is a growing body of evidence in support of the standard model. For example, the fact that aphasia affects users of sign language in exactly the same way counts as strong evidence. The standard model supports the modular view of a language faculty.

The holistic view seems to be supported by recent neurological research. According to clinical professor of psychiatry John Ratey of Harvard Medical School, 'We no longer see language as a highly localized function that exists in a neatly defined section of the brain. Indeed, language functions are distributed throughout the brain, and the locations can vary significantly from one person to the next' (2002: 253). There is no general headquarters where everything 'comes together'. Information is processed in different areas and activity is widespread.

  Yet despite the brain's plasticity and its significant variation from one individual to the next preventing a general model of the brain, Ratey argues that ninety-five per cent of *known* brain activity related to language use is situated in the left hemisphere. Figure 8 illustrates the positions of some of the main locations of language activity in the brain.

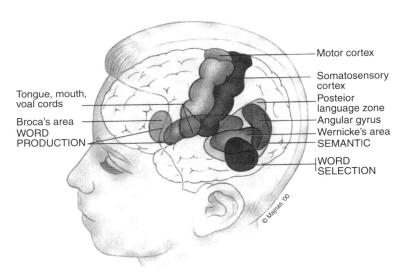

Figure 8 The Language Brain
Source: Illustrations by Hilda R. Muinos from THE USER'S GUIDE TO THE BRAIN by John Ratey, M.D., copyright © 2001 by John J. Ratey, M.D. Used by permission of Pantheon Books, a division of Random House, Inc.

So is language separate or not? The words 'a separate module' easily conjure up an image of a very particular location. Biolinguist Lyle Jenkins writes, the language module 'need not be exclusively identified with any particular localized area (e.g. Broca's area, Wernicke's area, etc.), but must be understood to include neural language circuitry with a possibly quite complex topological distribution' (2000: 65). In other words, the mechanisms of language are distributed and not a neat whole like, for example, the heart.

The notion of separateness also implies a degree of autonomy, but on closer reading we find that, 'Alongside the language faculty and interacting with it in the most intimate way is the faculty of mind' (Chomsky 1975: 35). The mind brings to bear upon language a whole array of other cognitive traits and capacities. So, even the boundaries of this module are notional. Where, then, is the 'syntax centre' of the language faculty? To his credit, Jenkins honestly admits that, at present, 'We have no neurology of UG [Universal Grammar] to draw from' (2000: 65).

Given our present state of knowledge, it is probably better to speak of 'language areas' rather than modules and bear in mind that this is another strand of the Chomskyan argument for rich innate cognitive structures for language. We will not know how separate the workings of these areas are until neuroscientists find out more about the brain, and it is this scarcity of facts that causes disagreement among the experts.

Is the Truth Hidden by Assumptions?

We have seen how words like 'module' can conjure up images that belie the truth and how bipolar contrasts can conceal the middle ground. But they are not alone. Words are not always our friends, they can mislead and misrepresent. Here's another that we need to be careful of – 'function'. It belongs to a select few that are fundamental to the way we describe our world. Let's be clear about its meaning.

Because the evidence suggests that language is confined to certain areas of the brain, many talk of these areas as having a special function. But there are broad and narrow definitions of 'function' and, unfortunately, writers do not always make it clear which they are using. Its broad meaning is synonymous to 'role' and 'use'. So in answer to questions like, 'What's language used for?' we could answer 'to communicate', 'to socialize', 'to think'. But these answers do not explain how these functions work, they are merely statements of use. An extension of this meaning is 'function' defined as 'purpose'. In sense 2, it moves closer to the notion of 'cause' and becomes more controversial because it purports to be an explanation. There is a third sense which emphasizes instrumentality – the contribution of a part to a controlling whole. And it is sense 3 that can mislead. If language is a module in the brain, it is tempting to think of it as the smaller part controlled by some higher cognitive centre. But there is no headquarters. Language would also have to make a *specific* contribution to our consciousness. It is argued by some influential linguists and philosophers that its role is to represent pre-existing, non-linguistic, 'pure' thought as language. And it is here that we need to be wary. In this context, sense 3 becomes a part of the modern argument for the separation of thought from language.

The argument for this separation has a long history. It reaches back to when the earliest philosophers of ancient Greece made the first step away from supernatural explanations. In their search for order in the natural world, they separated the underlying reality of things from their outward appearance. In time, this division would lead to another – the difference between things and their representations in the mind. All the time, in the background of their reasoning, was the belief that the observable, physical world was somehow more real, more objective, than the unobservable, subjective mental world. Following this path, they then separated thought from language. Representations were thoughts and speech was language. But if, as we have already argued, thoughts invariably come dressed in language, then this is a false assumption.

The modern argument for their separation has both language and thought in the mind, but as distinct forms of mental information. This is in spite of the fact that no one has yet been able to show that there are specialized brain areas for conceptual thought. One influential exponent of this argument Ray Jackendoff writes, 'Unlike language, music, vision, though, we have not been able to show that there are specialized brain areas for conceptual thought' (1994: 203). One senses the shaky foundations of their argument when they talk of 'a language of thought' or 'mentalese' and it all begins to sound like verbal acrobatics. In the absence of evidence, it would be better to consider language and thought as one, inseparable equals, neither controlling the other, co-existing in a hand-and-glove relationship.

Examining the role of language vis-à-vis the other four functions (sense 1) of the brain (movement, memory, emotion and social ability), Ratey writes that they permeate one another. In other words, they are all multi-functional. Even movement does not escape the embrace of language: 'Gesturing and speech are closely bound; they are acquired together in childhood and break down together in aphasia' (Ratey 2002: 270). It would seem that language is so utterly interwoven with other functions that its separation should be viewed more as a desire for a clearer explanation. It is how we objectify the world to make sense of it. But it is just possible that our natural desire for simple explanations may be leading us to mistake the map (our description) for the territory (reality).

If language is not controlled by any HQ and integrated with other mental functions, arising naturally and spontaneously with consciousness then it stakes out our existence as *expressive being*. No functions of the sense 2 and 3 kind, no divisions of thought and language, just a cognitive relation that has thinking-in-language as part of its knowing.

Summary

There are many different views on the relation of mind to language and language to thought. This chapter has merely indicated the tip of a very prickly iceberg.

To recap: language is a one-sound-at-a-time phenomenon that matches the way our attention mechanisms process sensory input; it is of a serial, sequential nature and uttered in bursts of sound that form contrasts at a basic phonemic level on an all-or-nothing basis; sound is the medium, the vehicle, that carries the sign outward to the listener; the signs are symbols that stand for things; some symbols fulfil a syntactic role by showing how both the outward string of acoustic signals as well as the inward images of sound are linked. These defining properties form the species-specific, universal characteristics of language; the details, the way names, values and meanings are attached to objects and events, are the settings that vary according to individual languages and are handed down to us through cultural transmission; the organization of language gives it the characteristics of a system; the system has a number of functions mainly of a social and communicative nature, but the conversion of thought is not one of them. They are one.

Chapter 2: We stated that language was unique to humans, but that there are links to the ways that some animals communicate. The most obvious were our nonverbal means of conveying emotion and feeling. We then considered how we use symbols to direct action. We found that instinctive, reflexive and conditioned behaviour was common. The use of language for reasoning, however, was far-removed from anything in the animal world. A general outline of consciousness was given and key properties of language were noted. Next, the question of whether language had a distinct location in the brain was considered. Although the evidence suggests that it has, we concluded that language is so inextricably woven into the fabric of mind that it would be better to keep an open mind on this question. Similarly, regarding claims that language and thought are separate, we thought it better to view them as inseparable until there was more evidence. There are other views regarding language's relation to consciousness that differ to the one presented here. The complexity of the subject admits no easy answer.

Study Questions

1. What do you think is the essential difference between two birds calling to one another and two people speaking?
2. Do you think our inner language is different to our spoken? If so, how? Offer examples.
3. Do you think we can think without using language? Give reasons for your opinion.
4. Do you think an exact location for language in the brain could ever be specified?

Chapter 3: We shall examine the connection between language and time.

Why Do Languages Change?

Introduction

Despite the universal constraints that our kind of consciousness places upon language, enormous differences exist between the world's six thousand odd languages. Some linguists play down these differences by describing them as variations on a single theme – human. Others think they stem, not from one source, but from the diversity that cultures exhibit. But all agree on one thing: languages do change over time.

The study of language change belongs to the field of **historical linguistics**, sometimes called **diachronic linguistics**. The technical term diachronic refers to the study of the processes of language change over time. Historical linguistics has three broad areas of enquiry. The first is the study of the history of particular languages on the basis of existing written data. **Comparative philology** used to do this, until it was gradually incorporated into the more scientific approach of historical linguistics from about two hundred years ago. The second area of enquiry is the study of the prehistory of language when there was no written evidence. The third area is the study of changes that are happening now. The latter approach is termed **synchronic**. Basically, synchronic studies look at the state of a language at a particular point or period of time, while diachronic studies consider the processes of change over time.

In this chapter, we shall focus on changes that stem from the passage of time. We shall begin by showing the scale of these changes and explaining some of the underlying processes. Then, we shall turn our attention to evolutionary explanations for language change and ask how Darwinian they really are. Lastly, we shall consider one large-scale change that radically altered English to the way we know it today.

The Scale of the Changes

Over large periods of time languages undergo so many changes that they become unrecognizable. Anyone who has been forced to study the classical form of a language at school would vouch for this. To give readers an idea of the scale of these changes, consider the following texts.

Beowulf is one of the four most important surviving manuscripts of Old English literature. The unknown author of *Beowulf* (*c.*1000) tells of a professional poet, or *scop*, who drawing on his 'word-hoard' tells the heroic tale of monster slayings in Scandinavia. The lines quoted beneath are Beowulf's dying words, commanding the construction of a barrow to his memory.

> Hata∂ hea∂oma re   hlæw gewyrcean
> beorhtne æfter bæle   æt brimes nosan;
> se scel to gemyndum   minum leodum
> heah hlifian   on Hronesnæsse,
> þæt hit sæli∂end   sy∂∂an hatan
> Biowulfes biorh,   ∂a ∂e brentingas
> ofer floda genipu   feorran drifa∂.

Most English speakers would not be able to read this or understand the reason for the gap in the middle of each line. There are letters such as ∂ (now 'th') and æ (now the /a/ as pronounced in 'hat') that have disappeared from the alphabet. There are also combinations of letters such as 'hl' and 'hr' that are no longer used. This is why Sanders provides a translation:

> Command the warriors famed in battle build a bright mound after my burning at the sea headland. It shall tower high on Whale Ness, a reminder to my people, so that seafarers may afterwards call it Beowulf's barrow when they drive their ships from afar over the dark waves. (1994: 21)

Almost four hundred years after *Beowulf,* English becomes more recognizable. The next extract is taken from the end of the *General Prologue* of Geoffrey Chaucer's *The Canterbury Tales* (*c*.1380).

> Whoso shal telle a tale after a man,
> He moot reherce as ny as evere he kan
> Everich a word, if it be in his charge,
> Al speke he never so rudeliche and large,
> Or ellis he moot telle his tae untrewe,
> Or feyne thing, or fynde wordes newe.

Although the spelling is different, we can recognize words such as 'untrewe' for 'untrue' and 'speke' for 'speak'. It is certainly easier to understand than the Anglo-Saxon of *Beowulf.* But we must be careful because the meanings of some familiar words may not be the same. For example, 'rudeliche' for 'rudely' was closer to 'coarsely' than 'impolitely'. And 'large' does not match its present-day meaning either.

By the time the Renaissance had reached England some two hundred years later, the language was blessed with the birth of a genius – William Shakespeare. His crafting of the English tongue would raise its prestige immensely. Here is a passage from *Twelfth Night*:

> Duke: [To Curio and Attendants] Stand you awhile aloof.
>   [To Viola] Cesario,
>   Thou know'st no less but all: I have unclasp'd
>   To thee the book even of my secret soul.
>   Therefore, good youth, address thy gait unto her,
>   Be not denied access, stand at her doors,
>   And tell them, there thy fixed foot shall grow
>   Till thou have audience. (Act 1, Scene 4).

This was first printed in 1623 and, although Shakespeare's metaphors still puzzle schoolchildren, the language is comprehensible to contemporary speakers of English. Differences abound, however, on all linguistic levels. For example, the second person singular of verbs still ended in '-st' as in 'know'st'. Singular personal pronouns like 'thou', 'thee' and 'thy' were still in use as well as prepositions like 'unto'. The word order is sometimes different, too. For example, 'Be not denied . . .' is unusual for us. Some phrases, such as 'address thy gait' meaning 'go', have also fallen out of use. Similarly, the meaning 'aside' for 'aloof' has changed.

The three texts are drawn from the three historical periods that English has been divided into. The first is from Old English (hereafter OE) which ran from approximately AD 450 to 1100. The second is from Middle English (hereafter ME) which followed and continued until 1500. The last belongs to Modern English, but to its early period which ran until 1750. The Late Modern English period runs to the present.

Although these texts, as well as the periods, may suggest that English developed in distinct stages, this is not true. Language change is a continuous process. There were no cataclysmic changes that announced the end of one period and the commencement of another. The changes were gradual, one period imperceptibly giving way to another. Though we scarcely notice it, language is changing all the time. This applies to all languages and is, therefore, a universal fact. Some abrupt, piecemeal changes, such as the appearance of a new word or a new usage for an existing word, may be conspicuous. Sea changes, however, can go unnoticed because they span generations and are very gradual. Historical linguist Herbert Schendl cites the disappearance of **case inflections** between Old English and Middle English as an example of a change that took hundreds of years (2001: 7). Case inflections indicate how the words of a sentence are related and we shall say more about them later. But, first, we shall look at the kinds of changes that can occur.

Two Kinds of Change

Two kinds of change are generally recognized – extra-linguistic and linguistic. Sometimes they are termed social and systemic. Are they related? Linguist Jean Aitchison thinks that social change may act as a catalyst that triggers off imbalances that were waiting to happen in the language system (2001: 151). But it is very difficult to say. This is because the mechanisms of change are complex and still not fully understood. Nor, as we shall see, are they as separate as one might think. Let's look at some examples that derive from extra-linguistic causes.

Extra-Linguistic Change

One kind of change that stems from extra-linguistic reasons are major historical events, such as invasions. Invasions introduce not just new sounds, but entirely different languages. In the case of English, foreign invasions introduced first Anglo-Saxon and then Norman French to southern England. It is no coincidence that the dates cited for OE and ME begin shortly after the arrival of Angles, Saxons and Jutes (*c.*449) and the Norman Conquest in 1066, respectively. Chaucer's English was the eventual fusion of these two tongues. In the ninth century, there was another wave of invaders – the Vikings. They took the north and east of England and were only halted when King Alfred of Wessex won a decisive victory in 878. A treaty was reached whereby the Danes retreated to the east of a line running roughly from Chester to London. The significance of this line, called the Danelaw, was that it helped sustain differences in dialect between the north and the south by preventing both sides from mingling.

Although the causes are not fully understood during the eighteenth century a major sound shift began. Later it came to be named the Great Vowel Shift. To understand it, we need to realize that the period that preceded it – Middle English – was a period of great variety. There was not just one language in England, but many. Linguist Jonathan Culpeper writes that while Latin was used for legal and scholarly texts, Norman French was the language of those governing the country. The governed spoke a variety of English dialects. They are sorted into five groups – Northern, West and East Midlands, Southern and Kentish. Within each of those dialects there would have been numerous local dialects. On top of this Celtic languages were spoken in Cornwall, Wales and Scotland. Against this confused background, the pronunciation of long vowels began to change in the Early Modern English period.

One example Culpeper offers is how the vowel of 'sweet' used to be pronounced like the vowel of 'set' except that it was longer, that's why there is a double 'e'. If you practise this pronunciation, you will feel the difference of where the sound is being made in your mouth. Basically, the vowel sound of present-day 'sweet' has shifted to the front and moved higher in the mouth. Culpeper summarizes the effects of the Great Vowel Shift as 'vowels articulated at the front of the mouth were raised and fronted, and vowels articulated at the back were raised and backed' (1997: 20).

In this, we see how small changes in the force of the articulation of a phoneme can have a knock-on effect. Interestingly, the sound system does not react in a haphazard manner, but works to establish a new symmetry of contrasts. If one sound shifts slightly, its opposite shifts in a manner that compensates.

Change is not always forced by invasions, or by dialects coming into contact with one another. In modern times, demographic changes, such as urbanization, have been cited as the main reason for the loss of, not just dialects, but whole families of languages. The trend of people to move from remote country regions to densely populated cities has fuelled this phenomenon. Whenever cultures or subcultures come into contact – an inevitable consequence of the movement of people – changes are likely to accelerate. But even if you do not move, the influence of great urban centres can be felt. Kent is a county that is just to the south and east of London. Once it had a dialect of its own, but today it has died out and been replaced by London speech.

In the examples cited above, it is clear that speakers are the prime movers of language change. This is why it is difficult to disentangle social from systemic change. Social change may originate from extra-linguistic causes of a political and economic kind, but it is carried, quite literally, in the mouths of speakers. Sometimes the speakers comprise the entire speech community of a feudal kingdom, other times they may be a particular social group within a modern state. The smaller the group is, the greater their influence must be to effect a change. In modern times, the media has provided the influence that can compensate for numbers. A good example is how a minority dialect, spoken by a very influential 3 per cent of the population, became the standard for English when it was adopted by the BBC for broadcasting in the early days of radio.

While some speakers are causing changes to occur, others are adapting to those changes. If the people running the country speak Norman French and you speak Old English, a form of German, then, like it or not, something is going give. But changes will occur naturally anyway. Younger generations will speak slightly differently to older generations. This suggests that if there is a unit of measurement for language change it will be the span of one generation. While all speakers understand the language of the community they grow up in, as time and geographical space extend the threshold of understanding is likely to diminish.

Let's now consider linguistic change.

Linguistic Change

Change can occur at different linguistic levels – spelling, sound, structure, word and meaning. Changes at every level can feed into others and effect further changes. For example, Renaissance scholars were very influenced by Latin and began to add 'h' to a number of Middle English words. Culpeper cites the following example: the Middle English word *trone* became 'throne' and its pronunciation changed from [t] to [θ] (1997: 13). Similar changes occurred in many other words. In this, we see how change to spellings affected pronunciation. At the lexical level, the borrowing and coining of new words for things or concepts foreign to our language is well documented. For example, linguist Larry Trask lists the following as examples of how English borrowed 'whisky' from Scots Gaelic, 'yogurt' from Turkish, 'tomato' from Nahuatl, 'sauna' from Finnish, 'ukulele' from Hawaiian and 'kangaroo' from the Guugu-Yimidhirr language of Australia (1999: 176). Similarly, how new words are made from existing words by adding prefixes or suffixes is also well covered in the literature. In what follows, we shall offer an example of linguistic change that may not be so familiar.

Syntactic Change

In recent years, linguists have become very interested in the principles underlying syntactic changes. They have isolated two mechanisms of such change. The first is the process of **grammaticization** (sometimes termed **grammaticalization**) and the second is **reanalysis**. We shall consider grammaticization first and reanalysis later.

Grammaticization

Grammaticization is considered more complex than reanalysis. It is a process whereby words that originally only had a lexical role gradually adopt a grammatical function. For example, originally, English 'will' meant 'want', as it still does in German. Gradually, it became co-opted for use as an auxiliary verb to indicate the future tense. This process often involves a narrowing of its semantic range (sometimes termed 'semantic bleaching') and a phonetic reduction. In the case of 'will', it was reduced phonetically to 'll, as in such sentences as 'I'll see you tomorrow'. Semantically, it was deprived of its original meaning 'want'.

Grammaticization in English frequently involves a similar transition from a main to an auxiliary verb. To illustrate this process, we shall look at how 'dare' came to be.

How 'Dare' Came To Be

'Dare' is a very old word, so to limit the scope of our investigation, we shall only consider its intransitive form, meaning 'to have boldness, courage' followed by an infinitive, as in 'He dared to enter the room'. In this sentence, 'dare' is a semi-**modal** (an auxiliary verb which expresses the attitude of the speaker). Typical modals are 'want', 'ought' and 'should', etc.

The chance event that introduced 'dare' to what would later become the English language was the invasion of Angles and Saxons from Northern Europe during the sixth and seventh centuries. In the *Oxford English Dictionary* (hereafter OED), its first recorded use is found in the *Lindisfarne Gospel c.*950. Its form and pronunciation then was different. Its first person present indicative form was 'dear' in the south and 'darr' in the north (Scotland). This form, as well as its second, third person, and past participle forms, had various spellings. The OED lists these variations. These variants should not be thought of as representing a progression towards a final form. Most people simply spelt words as they sounded in their dialect. The OED faithfully records these variants. Two main dialects are recorded in the OED – southern English and Scottish English. To keep things simple, we will only consider changes to the former in the first person present indicative form – 'I dare . . .'

The first southern form recorded was 'dear' in the year 1000, 'der' is recorded in 1205, then 'dar' in 1225, then it reverts to 'dear' in 1240, 'dar' is recorded again in 1350, 'der' also again in 1350, then in 1420 'dar' and, finally, by 1513, it appears to have stabilized

to its present form 'dare'. Significantly, this happens after the introduction of the printing press by Will Caxton in approximately
1476. Naturally, the existence of printed copy would have promoted standardization. According to the records, this process took
a minimum of 500 years, but a more likely figure is 800 years since
the records were written much later than the invasions.

In their studies of the mechanisms of language change Bybee
et al. (1994) write that when some lexical words become grammaticized (shift to a grammatical status) the likely processes are
(i) the lexical morpheme (in this case 'dare' and its variants)
becomes more frequent, (ii) the meaning becomes more abstract,
(iii) there is phonological reduction (that is, loss of stress or independent tone) and (iv) the word becomes more dependent on
context (that is, the words it can co-occur with become fewer).
Because 'dare' is a semi-modal, and not a full modal it may not
exhibit all of these features of grammaticization. But let's consider
each point in turn.

Did 'dare' and its variants become more frequent? The OED lists
three other verb and four other noun entries under 'dare' because
they share the same spelling. Of the three other verbs, one meant
'injure'. It became obsolete. Another meant 'to gaze fixedly or stupidly'. It, too, vanished: all four of its intransitive senses died out
between 1440 and 1540. Its two transitive meanings were obsolete
by 1860. This would have increased the frequency of 'dare' and,
more importantly, helped clear the way for its transition to grammatical status. OED's third listed verb with the same form as 'dare'
is a variation of 'thar', the old form of 'need' – another modal. Confusion may have prevailed because 'dar' (old 'dare') might have
been pronounced similarly to 'thar' (old 'need'). But 'thar', too,
vanished around 1460 leaving the road ahead clear for 'dare' to
become the only verb with that pronunciation.

The nouns show a similar story of gradual disappearance, but,
for the sake of brevity, we shall confine our comments to 'dare' as
a verb. We read in the OED the following comment, 'present "dare"
has been carelessly used for past "dared" or "durst" '. Clearly, chance

events in a social environment can come from any quarter, not just invasions, but also incorrect use. This is why 'dare' belongs to a small group of Teutonic verbs termed preterite-present whose present form was once mistakenly used as their past form.

What a journey of mishaps this single word must have had to reach us! It is particularly these senseless changes that illustrate the unoriented possibilities of variation. We also discover from OED's records that originally infinitives that followed 'dare' in its many earlier forms were not preceded by 'to'. This came later. OED says that using 'to' before the infinitive (e.g. 'dare to speak' and not 'dare speak') makes the utterance more emphatic. This seems the opposite to phonological reduction because it offers speakers a choice – emphatic or not. But when we come to consider **collocation** (the company that words can keep) we see that its range did become restricted. 'Dare' came to be used so often with 'say' that gradually it would be spelt as one word – 'daresay'. This 'daresay' is generally used in the first person singular or plural and the stress is restricted to the first syllable. This could be viewed as collocational restriction and a partial phonological restriction. OED has its meaning as 'I venture to say', but there's a modern pragmatic dimension where it means something like, 'I believe you, but it makes no difference'. Thus, a motorist stopped for speeding might say, 'I didn't realize I was going so fast' and a police officer might reply, 'I daresay you didn't, but you still have to pay a fine.' In this instance, it seems to have extended its meaning, but with other combinations it has not.

This single example of 'dare' acts as a cameo, allowing us to glimpse how chance events – invasions introducing different languages, rivalry between dialects, the absence of 'correct' spelling forms giving rise to many variants, an eventual tug-of-war between correct and incorrect forms once standardization is recognized as a goal, confusion at certain points in a word's history – lead to adaptation. And how, within these mechanisms of adaptation, processes of grammaticization create an apparent, though relative, stability in an area within the system of language. The elimination of weaker rivals occupying the same, or very similar, semantic or phonetic territory is particularly Darwinian.

The only constraint upon the development of 'dear' to 'dare' would have been its original meaning, as defined by use, and its sound. It could not have evolved, for example, from 'dear' to 'stun' or some other radically different sound associated with another meaning because the system of language would have resisted such a disconnected leap. Systemization represents a kind of rigidity. Within its web of constraints, we see the structure of language affecting its own possible paths of evolution.

Where redundancies appear in the system, change is likely to occur more rapidly. One reason for this has to do with efficiency or ease of communication – cumbersome expressions become an awkward 'mouthful'. Another reason is that systems, in general, can only tolerate a certain amount of redundancy. Here's one example, 'uprise above'. This verb crops up in Joseph Conrad's novels, although, doubtless, his contemporaries would have used it, too. Clearly, you do not need both 'up-' and 'above' with 'rise'. When the redundancy was removed, we were left with 'rise above'.

One would imagine that once conventions of spelling and printing are established, the pronunciation of words would stabilize. The conventions would act as a safe haven, protecting them from the volatile medium of air and all the individual idiosyncrasies of speech. This would be the case if spelling matched pronunciation. But we all know that this is not the case with English. The main reason for the phonemic mismatch was the adoption of an alphabet that was intended for a different language – Latin. English has over forty phonemes but only 26 letters to represent them. It also has about 20 different vowel sounds, but only five vowel letters. As a result, English pronunciation is as prone to change as ever it was.

Words not involved in grammaticization may not be subject to such a stormy passage through time, but, nonetheless, they will undergo changes, sometimes small, sometimes great, sometimes of form and other times of meanings. Here's an example of an exchange of views concerning the most unexciting of words.

In 'A Note on the Text' to George Orwell's classic novel *Nineteen Eighty-Four*, Peter Davison writes that Orwell's editor was horrified at seeing 'on' and 'to' printed as one word. He wrote to Orwell on the matter in 1949. Orwell was in hospital dying of tuberculosis at the time. He replied from his deathbed:

> As to 'onto'. I know this is an ugly word, but I consider it to be necessary in certain contexts. If you say 'the cat jumped on the table' you may mean that the cat, already on the table, jumped up and down there. On the other hand, 'on to' (two words) means something different, as in 'we stopped at Barnet and then drove on to Hatfield'. In some contexts, therefore, one needs 'onto'. (Orwell: xxi)

A very small change indeed, but coming from the pen of a great writer its use could hardly be dismissed.

It is tempting to think that the process of grammaticization is all there is to how 'dare' came to be and that there is nothing more to add: the system is simply making adjustments to itself. But this is very unlikely. The records are not the whole story. According to Schendl, there are three main explanations for language change – functional, psycholinguistic and sociolinguistic. He makes it clear that all of them could be contributing to change simultaneously, though not necessarily in equal measure. Let's consider these other explanations for language change.

Functional Explanations

Functional explanations focus on how changes internal to the system of language occur. Grammaticization belongs to this kind of explanation. In functional explanations, linguistic systems are seen as having a 'natural' tendency to regulate themselves. This self-maintenance is sometimes viewed as therapeutic – as if the changes were 'good' for the language. Critics are quick to point out that, if this were the case, languages would be evolving towards better design and that would contradict the earlier claim that the tendency was 'natural'. Darwin's explanation of natural selection is not teleological. In other words, nature is not working towards some goal, it is only adapting to changes. It is we who describe a change as 'better' or 'worse', and, when we do, it belongs to the small time-scale of our value system, not nature's.

Psycholinguistic Explanations

Psycholinguistic views focus on cognitive and psychological processes of language that go on inside a speaker's brain. These explanations are closely related to generative theories of language which believe humans are endowed with an innate faculty for acquiring language. It is argued that, as children grow, this faculty is activated and helps the child construct the correct rules for a mental grammar by exposure to language. But since this is not done perfectly, small differences arise. These minor deviations accumulate until a significant restructuring to the grammar occurs.

This explanation views language acquisition as the main reason for language change. It posits the source of most changes between generations. Among these explanations, some view grammatical changes solely in terms of formal rules that are independent of other linguistic and extra-linguistic factors. However, Schendl points out that there is ample evidence that syntactic change is not restricted to the time when children are acquiring language. It can, and does, occur among adult speakers (Schendl 2001: 71). This evidence comes from sociolinguistic studies and it is to their explanations we now turn.

Sociolinguistic Explanations

Sociolinguists have provided evidence by directly observing and recording change in progress. The idea of observing change in progress is relatively recent. It was instigated by William Labov in the 1960s in New York. Labov realized that the careful analysis of linguistic variation among different social groups might tell us a lot about the relation between a language's present state and its development through time. He discovered three important factors accounted for differences in speech among the groups studied – social class, formality of a situation and age. The absence or presence of certain words and expressions, termed **variants**, depended on these three factors. He interpreted the variation as an indication of change in progress and believed that it reflected a general trend over time.

As to the direction of change, he observed two different kinds. There were changes that move towards the established norms and there were changes which lead away from them. The first kind of change was carried mainly by women for whom the overt prestige of 'good' language was more important. The second kind was carried mainly by men for whom 'the covert prestige of non-standard varieties, especially those connected with working-class toughness, crude language, and group solidarity are more important' (Schendl 2001: 74). This finding cannot be generalized to all societies, however. Where the status of women is relatively fixed and there is no motivation for them to lead linguistic change, they do not.

Labov also believed that analysing differences between the speech of different age groups at one point in time would provide pointers for future change. If younger speakers were using a variant (e.g. 'No way', 'I'm good', or 'wicked', instead of 'great'), consistently and its frequency of occurrence was high, then it seemed reasonable to assume that it would replace the alternative used by older speakers. Alas, nothing is ever so simple. It seems that the speech of the young changes as they grow older and certain variants can vanish.

Unlike some psycholinguistic accounts, the sociolinguistic account acknowledges functional accounts of language change, although it treats them as secondary to social factors.

Summary

Schendl admits that there is 'still no generally accepted answer to the question of how and why languages change' (2001: 80). This suggests we should not think of grammaticization as the sole factor involved in how 'dare' came to assume a grammatical role. Instead, we should keep an open mind and recognize that many other factors probably played their part.

The fact that there is no clear answer is not really surprising. We mentioned earlier that there was something Darwinian about the process of how 'dare' changed over the centuries. One branch of historical linguistics argues an evolutionary account for language change. To some extent, this is the same as claiming that language change is 'natural'. In the next section, we shall ask how Darwinian this process is. In doing so, we hope to judge how 'natural' the process of language change is and understand why single, clear answers cannot be expected.

How Darwinian is Language Change?

Labov believed that variation was the basis of every linguistic change. Variation is also a key factor in Darwin's explanation of the origin of species. In other words, how there came to be so many different kinds of animals, plants and other living forms. In what follows, 'language' will be inserted into a brief account of Darwin's theory of natural selection to see how well it fits.

Darwin's explanation goes something like this: first, there must be a sufficiently complex pattern (a hedgehog, a human, a language). Second, the pattern must be copied. This is done for the organism by DNA by means of cell division. For language (opinions differ) by cultural transmission and/or innate acquisition. DNA occurs at the level of genes, for language (depending on your opinion) this would happen at a social (non-genetic) level, or, if you believe language is innate, a genetic level, or a combination of both these levels. If you believe in Dawkins's memes, the meme is the mind's copying unit working at a social level.

Next, small variations must occur to the pattern because of mistakes in copying the pattern. Selection is made among those variations. This occurs at the level of the body and its environment. This is the level at which nature plays her hand and why Darwin called his theory 'natural' selection. Whatever selections are made at this level will eventually, though not always, feed back down to the genetic level because changes will, if at all, be transmitted by inheritance. Although Labov recognized variation as the basis for every linguistic change, he also realized that not every variation leads to change. This is the same for living organisms: only those that are selected may lead to change within the population.

We saw earlier that variation in language can come from three main directions – the system, society and learning (copying) errors between generations. These directions form a linguistic and extra-linguistic environment. If changes to the system are triggered by extra-linguistic social factors, then the notion of environment comes closer to Darwin's explanation. If not, then it becomes more difficult to match up. There has to be at least two factors, one adapting to the changes in the larger environment. It could be argued that social groups within society meet this criterion.

The next important factor is that when variations occur the variants must compete. In nature, the variations compete for a limited work space. In the case of linguistic variants, the competition is in the mouths of speakers of different social groups. With language, if a variant assumes a social marking, it wins. It does not matter if it is uptown or downtown marking, if it has prestige, it wins. In nature, the competition is biased by the environment. If you keep mowing your lawn, it is unlikely the daisies are going take over from the grass. If there are big changes to the environment, then selection pressure increases and this speeds up evolutionary changes. Invasions, contacts with other cultures, could fall into this category of big environmental changes. But small biases in a multi-faceted social environment are very difficult to isolate while in progress.

In nature, there is a skewed survival or distribution that makes it possible for new variants to always occur preferentially around the more successful of the current patterns. It is at this point that our attempt to fit language into a Darwinian explanation grinds to a halt. Current patterns are hard enough to see let alone the linguistically more successful ones. Time reveals the winners, and time in Darwinian explanations is very long.

Lastly, the only variations that escape the original pattern are large ones. And they are few.

In this account, we can see numerous similarities but a complete matching of language change to biological evolution escapes us. This means we can only speak of language change as language evolution in the weakest sense. The reason it eludes complete correspondence is because language is artificial. Although it resides with us, and humankind are as natural a part of the Earth's environment as other living creatures, language does not grow as an arm does, or arrive as naturally as taste, touch, smell, sounds or sights to our senses. It needs the prompting of a social group that already uses it.

The main similarity is the tension between chance events forcing adaptations and the natural tendency for all things to gravitate towards patterns over time. This can be seen in both language as well as nature. Indeed, it's why language exhibits both variation and stability. It displays chance in the guise of variation and apparent law in the guise of patterns, often described as conventions or rules. These conventions represent agreements that have been won over time and which probably reflect a basic human desire for organization.

The reason we cannot expect simple, clear answers to language change is because the process that Darwin explained is both simple and, at the same time, mind-bogglingly profound. Of this process, physicist Paul Davies writes, evolution 'works by applying the filter of natural selection to blind variation on a moment-by-moment basis' and this is 'a random exploration of the available possibilities' (1998: 250). He uses the word 'happenstance' to characterize it. Where happenstance reigns, there is not going to be much room for principles that describe order and predictability. In similar vein, Ernst Mayr, a nobel-prize winning biologist, pinpoints another reason why there can be no single answers. Writing on how so few great thinkers have grasped the enormous power of variation and selection, he notes that the 'genotype-phenotype duality of the living organism is the reason why it is not sufficient in biology to search for a single cause in the study of a phenomenon, as is often sufficient in the physical sciences' (qtd. in Calvin 1996: 81). Life is not simple.

The One that Got Away

In the last section, we wrote that only large variations escape the original pattern. Let's look at one that changed the English language – the disappearance of **case inflections** between Old English (OE) and Middle English (ME). Case inflections are changes made to words to identify their relationship to other words in the sentence. The most common relationships are subject, object, indirect object and possession or origin. These were termed, respectively, nominative, accusative, dative and genitive. Words were also inflected to show if they were singular or plural, male, female, neuter and so on.

Consider the following oft-quoted example comparing Old German and OE which is drawn from Schendl (2001: 40).

Dem König gefielen die Birnen.
Dæm cyninge licodon peran.
'To-the-king pleased (the) pears.'
O (dative singular) – V (past plural) – S (nominative plural)

The first sentence is Old German, the second OE and the third a literal translation for both. The fourth indicates the order of the grammatical elements of the sentence: first, comes the object (O) followed by the verb (V) and subject (S). The noun phrases *Dem König* and 'Dæm cyninge' are singular indirect objects, hence the dative case. The verb is in the past tense and inflected to show that its subject ('the pears') is plural. In this way, inflections identified each word's relation to other parts of the sentence.

Here's another example. This one is drawn from David Crystal's encyclopedia of the English language (1995: 20).

The woman saw the man.
The man saw the woman.

In these two modern English sentences, the difference in the meaning is shown entirely by word order. In OE, however, they would have appeared, respectively, as follows:

1. Seo cwen geseah þone guman.
2. Se guma geseah þa cwen.
3. þone guman geseah seo cwen.

The female subject form 'seo' which means 'the' in 1 changes to the female object form 'þa' in 2. Similarly, the object masculine form 'þone' in 1 becomes subject form 'se' in 2. 3 has the same meaning as 1 regardless of the change in word order. It should not be difficult to glean from this that inflections form a complex network of agreements.

Gradually, the inflections to OE words were lost. Only then, did we get uninflected forms such as 'the king', 'the woman', 'the man' and so on which could stand as both subject and object without any change. In a similar fashion, OE verbs lost their inflections. In the first example, the '-on' of 'licodon' shows that it is not one pear but pears. When the verbs lost these inflections, English verbs became unmarked for number and person (except for the third person present tense, e.g. 'She goes'). Eventually, the typical ME word order became S-V-O. This, in time, led to a **reanalysis** of 'The king liked the pears' as having only one possible meaning – 'the king' as subject.

Reanalysis is another process of grammaticization. It makes it sound as if the speakers of a language are making conscious choices between alternative grammatical forms. This is highly unlikely. Norman French, like other French dialects, had already lost the case inflections Old French had inherited from Latin. Its uninflected forms probably competed with OE inflected forms and a number of social factors decided the outcome, not least the fact that the Normans were running the country.

These large-scale changes have a knock-on effect. Most interestingly, in the case we have outlined, the changes from O-V-S to S-V-O show a predictable pattern. Schendl writes, 'Languages with the basic order V-O share other certain word order patterns and grammatical features which tend to have precisely the opposite value in OV languages' (2001: 41). Languages with a typical order of object-following-verb will have auxiliary verbs in front of main verbs (e.g. 'I must go'), comparative adjectives before nouns (e.g. 'a faster car'), and prepositions before nouns (e.g. 'from him'). On the other hand, languages with a typical order of verb-following-object have the exact reverse. When a language changes its basic order from VO to OV, or vice versa, it often changes all or most of the above characteristics accordingly. It is tempting to see in this an invisible hand – the system of language reacting to changes in a logical manner as if in isolation. But two, or more, forms usually co-exist for a long time before one yields to the other.

Conclusion

The flux that language exists in is time. Within its vastnesses, the clash of two titans Chance (random events) and Order (events that have gradually fallen into a pattern) create friction. Friction sets in motion processes of adaptation. The results are temporary fixes that represent a brief respite from the struggle between Chance and Order. Force of habit aids patterning and order. While patterning can occur at both genetic and social levels, it is highly unlikely that changes at the social level filter down to become encoded at the genetic. There is no need for this to happen because language can be transmitted culturally. Its inheritance by successive generations forms the pattern that Darwin termed 'descent with modification'. The way a language is at a certain point in time is the accumulation of its adaptations to past events. All its quirkiness, as well as its regularities, are the product of the past. Borne on the waves of successive generations, it comes to lap, gently murmuring, at the edge of each newborn's consciousness.

Chapter 3: We looked at the scale of changes to language over time and then the underlying causes. These divided into linguistic and extra-linguistic and were of a systemic or social nature. Two kinds of systemic change were considered: grammaticization and reanalysis. Both belong to functional explanations of language change. There are other explanations and two – psycholinguistic and sociolinguistic – were outlined. We concluded that all make contributions to change and that the process of change is so complex that it defies a simple explanation.

Study Questions

1. Can you think of any words that have changed or extended their meanings in your lifetime?
2. Can you think of any words that are pronounced differently in another dialect of English?
3. If 'every word has its own history' as those who study dialects believe, do you think it is impossible to discover any regular patterns of language change?
4. Etymology is the study of the origin and history of words. Take an etymological dictionary, such as the *Oxford English Dictionary* or the *Concise Oxford*, and look at the history of words such as: 'weird', 'bead', 'crayfish' and 'postillion', or any other words that take your fancy. Tell each other what you found.

Chapter 4: In the next chapter we will look at language variation caused by cultural differences.

How Does Language Vary across Cultures?

Historical Background

In the first half of the twentieth century, language study was predominantly cultural and its focus was on communication. One of the reasons for this focus on communication was that many linguists were working in the field describing unknown languages. In effect, they were understanding language through the observation of communicative behaviour. During the second half of the same century, the situation began to change. Linguistics became more specialized and its focus more theoretical. As its interest began to shift away from the cultural, younger disciplines such as **anthropology** (study of people, society, culture) and **semiotics** (study of sign systems) began to fill the void.

Partly in recognition of this, one of the great linguists of the last century the Russian Roman Jakobson (1896–1982) proposed a three-tier approach to what he characterized as communication studies. He placed the study of communication of *verbal* messages in the field of linguistics, the study of communication of *any* message in the field of semiotics, and the study of communication in its *broadest sense* in the field of cultural or social anthropology, jointly with economics, where the communication of messages is implicit (1990: 463). By doing so, Jakobson acknowledged that communication could be studied at different levels – linguistic, social and cultural. This order moves from the specific study of the communicative aspect of language to how it can be treated as one of many communication-systems to how it can both express and embody culture. Figure 9 illustrates these connections. The words inside

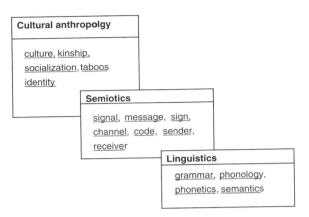

Figure 9 An inter-disciplinary approach to communication studies

each frame indicate some of the topics of each discipline and the smaller size of the semiotic and linguistic frames, the narrowing of focus from the general to the specific study of communication.

Since Jakobson proposed this multi-track approach, there have been a number of significant developments. The first was the establishment of **sociolinguistics** (the study of language in society) during the 1970s. Its focus of study is speech variation due to factors such as social class, age or gender. Sociolinguistics also concerns itself with language contact, language planning and social identity. Closely related is a branch of **sociology** (the study of society) called **sociology of language**. The latter studies the influence upon social action of general social and cultural processes, especially where they involve social class, ideology and distribution of power. These disciplines are fundamental to an understanding of communication in the context of culture.

This chapter considers cultural anthropology, sometimes referred to as **ethnology**. The linguistic focus of this field is 'language variation and use *in relation to* human cultural patterns and beliefs' (Crystal 1997a: 20). Let's begin by looking at the bonds that hold language and culture together.

Cultural Anthropology

The way in which linguistic features reveal the cultural patterns and beliefs of a society is well evidenced. One of the most famous anthropologists, the Frenchman Claude Lévi-Strauss (b. 1908), gives numerous examples of how proper names show various kinds of kinship relationships as well as the social organization of early communities in his classic *The Savage Mind*. But we do not have to go into the rain forests of Papua New Guinea or the deserts of Australia to find examples. Numerous examples can be found in modern societies, too. Let's take Japan as an example.

Students of Japanese would be struck at how many personal pronouns they have compared to English. For English 'I', there are *watakushi, watashi, atashi, boku, ore, jibun* and many children use their own proper names in place of 'I'. An observer might also notice how, despite this wide choice, once it is clear who the grammatical subject of a sentence is, Japanese tend to avoid their use in conversation. If they have to refer to another person, they prefer to use names or titles. In stark contrast, 'I' and 'you' are two of the most frequently occurring words in English conversation.

Some Japanese have remarked to me that when they first started using English, they hesitated to refer to someone who was present as 'you.' One equivalent for 'you' in Japanese is *anata*. Its spoken use is very specific. A wife can use this term to refer to her husband, an older man to a lower-ranking colleague, but there are many situations in which it is totally inappropriate. Similarly, the usage of *kare* and *kanojo*, the respective Japanese equivalents for 'he' and 'she', is very different. Sometimes *kare* and *kanojo* behave like nouns and mean 'boyfriend' and 'girlfriend'. At other times, usually when written, they refer to a third person whose name is not known, or, if known, to convey psychological distance. In addition to this, the choice of personal pronoun in Japanese can indicate whether the person is male, female, an in- or out-group member, and of a higher/lower social status.

What can be deduced from these differences? It points to cultural differences with regard to the **speech acts** (a subset of social actions) of naming and addressing. Not all differences between languages reveal cultural divergence, however. Some may seem to be unrelated to culture and only of a grammatical, lexical or phonetic kind. Before considering other intercultural differences, let's remind ourselves of the intricate connection between languages and their own culture.

The Nexus between Language and Culture

We are all born into a time, and we all inherit the cultural view of that period. It is a view that is at work in the background of every situation. For example, I walk into a pub (I know this place sells ale). I go to the bar to order a beer (I know no one will serve me if I sit down at a table). I order a particular beer (I know there's a choice) and pay for it (I know I have to pay before, not after, I drink it). It is a perfectly ordinary situation for those who have grown up with it, but could not be so for those who have never heard of, let alone been to, a pub. The known is so taken for granted by members of the same culture that it usually goes unnoticed and unremarked. In linguistics, these background factors are termed **ontological assumptions**, but it is probably easier to think of them as the shared background understanding of a language community. How apt that the background to the spoken should be the unspoken.

This sharing of background knowledge amounts to sharing cultural values. These values help to bring order and predictability into people's use of language by creating norms that make people's actions more readily intelligible. Without these norms, misunderstandings would arise, possibly to the point of threatening the ease and efficiency of communication. Members of a speech community get to know these background values through socialization. This is accomplished through upbringing and schooling in the broadest sense of the word. In short, just being where you grow up.

This internalization of values serves to distinguish between the roles of society and culture which are often confused. Society institutionalizes the norms and values of culture in order to orientate its members towards common goals. Culture runs like a river through each successive society, its currents becoming ever deeper and more varied as time passes. Its most fundamental values can be traced back to religion. They are usually about what is right and what is wrong. Each society passes on those values so that its members share common goals. It is against, and within, this framework that communication functions.

As time passes, changes occur, not only to the meanings of words, the sounds of the language and parts of its grammar, but also to the values and beliefs that shape the cultural framework. Victorian moral values gave way to present-day standards, new inventions began to change the environment, and socio-political events changed the map of the world. The mutual interaction between society and language is easily shown. One example will suffice to show this. In the early 1970s, the British government decimalized the currency. Overnight, words that applied to the coins of the old money system – 'half-crown', 'shilling', 'threepence', 'sixpence', etc. – became redundant. New words for the new coins and notes of the decimalized currency became the norm. In other words, new systems, games, sports, inventions and so on, introduce new words and, sometimes, existing ones become obsolete.

Among the multitude of events forcing change to both language and the way we think, we shall select two. The first is technology and the second translation.

Technology – Cultural Artefacts

Technology has introduced an entirely new dimension to the dynamics of linguistic change. Telephone, radio, cinema, television, internet chat rooms, e-mail, etc. have enabled language to disseminate right across the globe and, among other effects, aided the process of standardization.

Among these inventions, radio's effect on spoken language was enormous – it began a linguistic process of levelling by introducing **prestige dialects** that many listeners would imitate. For example, early BBC radio broadcasters spoke a kind of public school English – a minority dialect. But so influential were these worldwide broadcasts that listeners copied this kind of English, with certain modifications, which is why it later became known as 'received pronunciation' (or simply, RP).

Today, television has replaced radio as the global dialect leveller. Linguist Stephen Fischer remarks how, in the 1970s, New Zealand knew nothing of American **discourse fillers** such as 'like', 'sorta', 'kinda', 'ya know', etc. By the mid 1990s, American TV programming had changed all that (1999: 174).

New technology always ushers in changes to a language, whether it is Norman longbows or Victorian steam engines. In our lifetime, computer technology has spawned thousands of new words – *database, download, online, broadband, website* – and added many new meanings to existing words, for example, *crash, freeze, mouse* and *cursor*.

The creation of new technology is usually a collective endeavour that affects language by changing our physical environment. But changes can come from individuals and be of a non-physical kind, too. Many new ideas enter the language via translation. Let's now turn our attention to how translation affects both ideas and language.

Translation

Rather than consider those colossal works of translation, such as the Bible, whose far-reaching effects are well documented, we shall look at more common, though less recognized, work. Broadly speaking, there are two kinds of translation – commercial and literary. We shall focus on the latter since another meaning of 'culture' is 'art'. Some translators do literary translation on order, that's to say for money. In such cases, it is often the chief editor of a publishing company who decides which books should be translated. But some translators do it for love, not knowing whether their work will ever be published.

Specific problems involved in the task of translation will depend upon the language pair, but, at the most general level, a question that is often asked is, 'Is translation possible?' It is generally recognized that an exact reproduction is impossible and probably not desirable. Most translators try to shape their work to the requirements of the target language. Only in this way can the translation evoke a new response. Another question typically discussed by translators is, 'What exactly is translation?' According to Michael Emmerich, a translator of Japanese, the commonest answer is that it is a kind of bridge-building, an attempt to span two cultures. This metaphor matches the meaning of the Latin *translatus* from which we get our word. The Latin means 'carried across' and implies the movement of one thing to another place. Emmerich thinks the metaphor contributes to the feeling that translation is doomed to fail (2007: 5). How can anyone, he wonders, possibly link separate cultures. There are simply too many differences.

This last point brings us to another question that is often on the lips of translators – the inevitability of loss. Nowhere is this felt more than in the translation of poetry or dialect. Poetry is dependent on sound and form for its effect, and, naturally, of all linguistic elements, these are bound to be lost in translation. So what do translators of poetry do? According to Janine Beichmann, a translator of Japanese poetry, they have to put a lot back in to compensate for the loss. She calls it a blood transfusion. She offers a number of examples which illustrate just how extraordinarily difficult the task is, but rather than cite examples which the reader may find difficult, we shall switch our focus to what can motivate these unsung heroes.

The driving force behind their work seems to be more like a fate, more a 'have to' than a 'want to'. They love the beauty that the poem holds so much that they are compelled to tease it out and re-dress it in their own tongue. That transfusion of new blood requires, among many other things, the search for evocative words, re-springing the poem's rhythm, and rearranging its shape upon a page. Beichmann writes how, when earlier Japanese translators brought home their work from Europe, not only did it become an inspiration for poets, it also changed their native tongue (2007: 4). It subtly altered the linguistic landscape, forever.

This last point leads to a final question: what would a language that had no foreign tributaries running into it be like? Would it be impoverished? To answer this, we would have to go back to a less populated age when there was little cultural exchange and no lines of telecommunication. Let's try the Greek city of Miletus on the Turkish coast 2,600 years ago. In Professor Guthrie's meticulous account of the thought of the earliest Greek philosophers of that period, we encounter some answers. First, he writes that the only literature they were acquainted with was poetry (1962: 118), mainly that of Hesiod and Homer. Concerning their struggle to express new ideas, he tells us that certain concepts, such as 'potentiality' or 'latency', were not fully understood 'as it was expressed in the crude language of the time' (1962: 87). He says that they did not have 'the latter-day advantage of reading in a variety of tongues' (1962: 118). He also discerns reasons for the difficulty of expressing those entirely original concepts – concepts that would eventually lay the foundations to Western rational thought – in the nature of their language. For example, how there was only one word for 'same' and 'similar' (1962: 230), and the way adjectives were combined with articles (e.g. 'the hot', 'the unlimited'). The latter made it appear as if the quality and the thing were one and so tended to conceal differences between the abstract and the concrete (1962: 242).

His account provides evidence that new concepts were extracted with the greatest difficulty, one, because the language had had little contact with others, two, because of the newness of the concepts and three, because of the structure of the language itself. The evidence is clear even from this distance of time. It strongly suggests that languages are enriched by the inroads of translation. Translation has the same effect as a stone dropped into a pond: it causes ripples to radiate outward, first changing the surface and then sinking beneath to become part of the pond.

Let's now turn our attention to the variation found among languages.

Language Variation

When we come to compare how different languages represent, not just the details of their cultures, but those aspects of reality that we all experience, regardless of place of birth, we find that, even here, the differences appear as arbitrary as the different sounds used for their expression. Let's take two examples – time and differences between male/female speech.

Time

We all experience time. We all see the same sun rise and fall, and we all live and die. These facts are universal, yet different languages represent them differently. Commenting on this, linguist Roy Miller writes:

> Time, like everything else in the real world, becomes available to linguistic systems only after it has undergone segmentation; moreover, that segmentation is apparently always carried out along lines that are quite as arbitrary, and quite as impossible to

predict or generalize across the lines of linguistic divisions and demarcations, as is any of the other linguistic evidence for arbitrary segmentation. (1986: 144)

Miller offers several examples. The first is how, in Russian, chronological time is not the only factor that affects the linguistic description of time. Much more important to the conjugation of verbs seems to be whether an activity or action is or was carried out to completion (1986: 148). This is termed **aspect** in linguistics and it represents a complicated and separate network of semantic relationships connected to **tense**. He shows how even languages that are related to one another historically can, and do, differ strikingly in their segmentation of time. He offers examples of how German uses the past perfect tense more than English and how its aspectual uses differ in terms of degree of completion of an action.

Linguist Michael Halliday has suggested that there are two basic models of time expressed by language. One is linear where everything comes out of the past via the present into the future. English is of this sort. The other kind expresses simultaneity and is more interested in the opposition between being and becoming, or manifested and manifesting (2003: 118). Japanese verbs are similar to this. They seem to be more concerned with whether or not an action or state is continuous, completed or incomplete, than past or not. The problems, however, are in the details. Languages do not fit neatly into either model, they can express both concepts but usually one is more dominant. It is hard to pinpoint the differences, but the following examples illustrate how, in Japanese, English present perfect, future and present continuous tenses can be lost in translation.

1. 'Hurry up! The game has already begun.' (English present perfect tense)
   「早く！試合はもう始まっているよ。」 'Hayaku! Shiai wa moo hajimatte iru yo.' (Japanese – te iru form. Literally: Hurry up! Game already starting/going on.)

2. 'That was definitely the best film I've seen this year.' (English present perfect tense)

「あれは今年観た中で間違いなく一番の映画だ」 'Are wa kotoshi mita naka de machigainaku ichiban no eiga da.' (Japanese non-past plain form of copula. Literally: That this year seen without doubt best film is.)

3. 'I'll be there at 3-o-clock sharp.' (English future tense)

「３時きっかりに待っています」 'Sanji kikkari ni matte imasu.' (Japanese – te iru form. Literally: 3-o-clock exactly am waiting.)

4. 'He's getting old.' (English present continuous tense)

「あの人は年をとったね。」 'Ano hito wa toshi o totta ne.' (Japanese past tense. Literally: He's got old.)

In example 2, a student told me that if she had just seen a movie, she would use the Japanese past tense. It is comments like these that reveal just how difficult it is to find examples that hold good in every conceivable situation. Languages are very context-sensitive.

Let's pause for a moment and consider the word 'arbitrary'. This word is used to describe something that does not appear to be based on any principle, plan, known criteria, or have any connection to nature. Are these differences among tenses as culturally determined as, for example, the personal pronouns mentioned earlier? Clearly, they do not reveal their links to their cultural background as obviously. The reasons that underlie their origins are usually so far removed from the present that they are unknown and, as a result, the structuring of time is described as arbitrary. But I don't think we should imagine from this that their formation was the upshot of pure chance.

Kindaichi, one of Japan's most respected linguists, basing his comments on some of the oldest extant literature in the world, wrote the following about the disappearance of the conclusive form of Japanese verbs in favour of the attributive. Towards the end of the Heian Period [794–1185], 'people began to feel that a sentence ending in the conclusive form was too cut-and-dried' (1978: 213). How should we interpret 'people began to feel'? I think we should understand 'people' as the writers of that period whose works survived because they were admired. In this, we recognize the power of script: spoken language is too restricted and ephemeral to effect such a change. It was the persistence of the *presence* of the works of a small group of writers over several generations that set in motion a trend away from the conclusive form by establishing an aesthetic preference for the attributive form. So reasons do exist, but often they are so far removed from the present that they become speculative and leave us little choice but to describe them as arbitrary.

Could the opposite of such a situation exist? Could languages not be arbitrary, but have natural connections? If they were, logically, they should all sound the same since the connections between words and the natural things they named would be clear. But words like, 'the', 'if', 'justice' and 'unicorn' do not name anything natural. Clearly, most of language has to be arbitrary since words are used not only for naming the real, but also for showing relations among themselves, abstract concepts and imagined entities.

Male/Female Speech

Every society has both men and women and there is no reason why they should speak differently unless, at some point in the past, a custom arose to accentuate gender differences. Such must have been the case in many societies. In Japan, for example, there are numerous differences between male and female speech, particularly in informal situations. These differences apply to asking questions, giving orders and a whole range of other language functions. I shall describe one difference which is very noticeable and easy to explain – the use of **particles**.

In Japanese, particles are used to indicate the grammatical properties of a sentence. For example, 'wa' shows the topic of the sentence, 'ga' its subject, 'o' the object of the verb, 'ni' the indirect object among other uses, and so on. But when they are used at the end of a sentence they can express the speaker's emotion or attitude. Of these sentence-final particles, some are used exclusively by men and others exclusively by women. Consequently, they mark the gender of the speaker. For example, 'yo', 'zo' and 'ze' are used by men when speaking informally to emphasize whatever has been said. Roughly, they correspond to English phrases such as 'I tell you', 'you know', 'I'll say', etc. For example,

（僕は）知らないよ。/ (Boku wa) shiranai yo. / I don't know.

The brackets indicate parts that may not be uttered in situation. In this example, if the 'don't' were stressed in English, it would equate with 'yo' or, if not stressed, then a 'do I?' tagged onto the end would do the same. Here are two more examples:

俺（は）負けないぞ。/ Ore (wa) makenai zo. / I won't lose!
これは金だぜ。/ Kore wa kin da ze. / Hey, this is gold!

A particle often used by women at the end of a sentence is 'wa'. It can express a light, almost playful, assertion. For example,

きれいだわ。/ Kirei da wa. / It's lovely.

This particle can combine with others such as 'ne' or 'yo'. For example:

行くわよ。/ Iku wa yo. / I'm going, too.
すてきだわね。/ Suteki da wa ne. / Isn't it wonderful!

In informal speech, women have a question marker of their own 'no'.

どうして泣いているの？/ Doshite naite iru no? / Why are you crying?

In formal speech, this 'no' would be followed by 'desu ka?'

There are countless other examples, but perhaps the reader is wondering why this is necessary when the gender of the speaker must be obvious. The reasons are partly related to aesthetic notions about what 'society' deems to be manly or feminine. Naturally, when we start to think about the customs of other cultures problems crop up because our own values enter the picture. For instance, suppose a commentator claimed these gender differences were instituted by a politically male-dominated society and are totally sexist, but then found out that neither gender was aware of any prejudice in their use. Could the commentator draw any legitimate conclusions?

Let's now look at the levels which culture is thought to operate at.

Three Levels of Culture

Most sociolinguists agree that culture has a double effect on individuals – it *liberates* them from the anonymity of nature by *imposing* a structure and principles of selection. This effect is revealed at social, historical and metaphorical levels. Let's consider each in turn.

The Social

At the social level, it is not only differences of grammatical, lexical and phonological features that differentiate members of the same speech community. Young people will have their own particular way of speaking and their topics of conversation will also be different. The way a person speaks at work and at home may be different. At work their language may be more polite, while at home they may use their own **idiolect** (personal manner of expression). The changes a person makes to their style of speech (**register**) is termed **code-switching** in linguistics. Differences in the style of speech, the topics people choose to talk about, the manner of their interaction is termed **discourse accent** and its study **discourse analysis**. Both are concerned with social interaction and integration.

In some languages, there is an elaborate system of honorific language – Burmese, Korean and Japanese, for example. In Japanese, this system is called *keigo*. Basically, when speaking, a choice is made regarding the degree of politeness deemed necessary. The choice is based on the status of the speaker relative to the listener/s and the context of the situation. This is why many Japanese exchange business cards when meeting for the first time. They can check the position of the other person in his or her company. Verbs are only one aspect of *keigo*, but the use of honorific verbs (*sonkeigo*) elevates the addressee, while the use of humble verbs (*kenjoogo*) lowers the addresser's status and so achieves the same effect. Distance between the addresser and addressee is created by the use of *keigo*, and this is a prerequisite for showing respect. People who cannot use *keigo* properly are deemed (usually by those who can) to be socially inept. But there is a dark side to use of *keigo*, it can be used to establish a safe distance from frankness or personal enquiry. Many employees of Japanese firms are taught to follow the 'manual' when speaking to customers. Although this is described as respectful, it can result in an impersonal, almost robotic, language.

The reasons for both code-switching, speech levels and a whole range of other sociolinguistic phenomena are found in sociological theories. Code-switching is about how individuals show their affiliation to certain groups by adopting the same manner of speech as other members. It is a statement of identity. The existence of speech levels generally reflects a society that was once stratified according to gender, class and profession and has not yet sloughed off the linguistic vestiges of that past. Both phenomena show that language, behaviour and society are inextricably bound.

The Historical

The historical level of culture concerns the cultural identity of the members of a speech community. Language is a system of signs that is seen as having a cultural value in itself. Speakers identify themselves and others through their use of language and view their language as a symbol of their social identity. In this sense, language symbolizes cultural identity: language can do this because it embodies it in its expression. This is partly why certain countries have established academies to protect their language which they view as part of their cultural treasure. Probably, the best known is the *Academie Francaise*. Set up in 1635 to establish Parisian French as the standard dialect, it remains today to stop French from becoming 'tainted' by foreign tongues, especially English.

It is interesting to note that once words have been assigned to particular objects, actions and events against a conceptual background of common assumptions and expectations, members of the community then find it difficult, if not impossible, to say anything entirely original about their view of the world. For example, once 'a bouquet of roses' has been codified by society to represent a way of expressing love, it becomes hard to choose different flowers to express the same.

Writers and poets are more concerned than most with breaking the mould of connotations and allusions that have attached themselves to certain words. William Blake (1757–1827), for example, created a whole new pantheon of gods in poetic works such as *The Book of Urizen*, *The Book of Ahania* and *The Book of Los* in order to escape the stultifying grip that he believed the Greek, Roman and Judaic mythologies had imposed on the minds of the public of his time.

The Metaphorical

The metaphorical level of culture is concerned with how speech communities are characterized not only by facts and artefacts, but also by common dreams and fulfilled and unfulfilled imaginings. Cultural anthropologist Claire Kramsch writes that these imaginings are mediated through the language that over the life of the community reflects, shapes and becomes a metaphor for its cultural reality. I understand this to mean that much of the imagery found in languages is culture-dependent. For example, in English we might say someone was 'born with a plastic spoon in their mouth', or that we were 'browned off', or that something acted as 'a barometer of our times'. But it is unlikely that other languages will use the same images for the same meanings. People who have studied a foreign language know that such idioms rarely keep their meaning when translated literally.

Because these images are not consistent across cultures, they are difficult for students of foreign languages. For example, once I heard a Japanese describe a woman entering a room 'like a jellyfish'. I thought the image had to do with the pulsing movement of jellyfish and my imagination took me to a tentative translation of 'she flounced into the room'. I discovered later that I was mistaken: it was not the jellyfish's movement, but its ghostly transparency that was the gist of the simile, and so 'she entered like a ghost' was correct. These differences are not usually found in bilingual dictionaries.

The term used in linguistics to describe the natural choice of vocabulary is **markedness**. Linguists Waugh and Monville-Burston write that markedness 'is also frequently associated with ideas of normality, regularity, predictability, and frequency of occurrence' (qtd. in Jakobson 1990: 41). So, in English, when we want to know someone's age, we ask, 'how old', not 'how young.' Or, if we want to know the height of something, we ask 'how tall' or 'how high', not 'how short' or 'how low'. In these examples, 'old', 'tall' and 'high' are marked, and the opposite member of this binary opposition 'young', 'short' and 'low' are, in these instances, unmarked.

There are, naturally, numerous differences (as well as similarities) between languages with regard to markedness. Here are three common examples between English and Japanese.

1. 'I didn't get out of bed till ten this morning.'
   「けさは１０時まで寝ていた。」 'Kesa wa juuji made nete ita.'
   'I carried on sleeping till ten this morning.'
2. 'You can keep it.'
   「返さなくていいですよ。」 'Kaesanakute ii desu yo' 'You don't have to return it.'
3. 'I can't remember.'
   「忘れました。」 'Wasuremashita.' 'I've forgotten.'

The differences are invariably more noticeable, but all instances reveal a preference for one lexical or grammatical expression over another. The choice does not operate like an absolute rule, but more like a default setting. The totality of such differences has led some to argue for **linguistic relativity** – the view that people think differently because their language offers them different ways of expressing the reality around them.

Linguistic Relativity

The best known version of linguistic relativity is the **Sapir-Whorf Hypothesis**. Historically, this thesis was formulated at a time when many native American languages were being studied. Franz Boas's (1858–1942) pioneering work describing these languages was taken up by his students, most notably Edward Sapir (1884–1939) and his student Benjamin Whorf (1897–1941) who gave their names to the hypothesis.

They held that there is such a strong interdependence between language, culture and thought that they essentially mirror one another. Arguing that language filters the way we perceive and categorize experience, Sapir wrote: 'We see and hear and otherwise experience very largely as we do because the language habits of our community predispose certain choices of interpretation' (1949: 162). And Whorf 'the world is presented in a kaleidoscopic flux of impressions which has to be organized by our minds – and this means largely by the linguistic systems in our minds' (1956: 212–213).

Commenting on 'the act of a stone falling,' Sapir pointed out how different languages describe this event differently: German and French are compelled to assign 'stone' to a gender category; Chippewa cannot express it without stating that the stone is inanimate; English has to state whether a stone, or any other object, is conceived in a definite or indefinite manner, is it 'a stone' or 'the stone'; the Kwakiutl Indian of British Columbia indicates whether the stone is visible or invisible to the speaker at the moment of speaking, and whether it is nearest the speaker, the person addressed, or some third person; the Chinese seem to get on quite well with a minimum of description, just 'stone fall' (1949: 157–159).

From this, we can see that different languages encode different information, sometimes grammatically sometimes lexically. It is difficult to judge from these examples, as well as those offered earlier on time and gender differences, the extent to which they reflect differences of thought. Do, for example, those differences of how time is grammaticized by languages really affect how people conceptualize time? Or are they just different ways of saying the same thing? Whorf thought that language does not affect all thought, only that there is cultural determination of *habitual thought*. Although he did not manage to draw a clear line between habitual thought and other kinds of thought, it seems a reasonable assumption and one that people who have lived in a different culture would support. For example, one notices how it is not just about differences of expression, but also about what topics are thought appropriate or not. So caution is needed: although language, culture and thought may reflect one another, they are not perfect mirrors of one another.

In the late 1990s, sociolinguists proposed a view that acknowledged both the universal and particular aspects of language. This weak relativistic standpoint argued that such differences do not preclude speakers of one language understanding the concepts of another language. If it did, they argued, translation would scarcely be possible. In its weak version, then, the notion that different world views are mutually inaccessible to non-native speakers is rejected. This watered-down version smacks somewhat of political correctness. It seems to want us to believe that everyone's view of the world is essentially the same, as if differences were bad.

Clearly, Sapir and his contemporaries held a very different opinion to today's generative linguists. They argued a variationist account of language derived from cultural diversity. Those who argue against the variationist account search for **language universals** (properties common to all languages) in the belief that these will reveal the fundamental similarities between languages. Let's look at some of the different kinds of universals that have been found.

Language Universals

The first and most obvious similarity between all languages is that they are organized – they form systems comprising sub-systems of grammar, lexicon and phonology that are regulated by rules. The search for unchanging universals within that broad framework began in earnest in the 1960s when the American anthropological linguist Joseph Greenberg set up a major project at Stanford University. It led to a seminal paper listing 45 universals. These universals take the form of statements such as: every language distinguishes between nouns and verbs; every language distinguishes at least 3 persons; every language has at least 3 vowels. These were termed substantive universals, while others were termed near universals because there were a few exceptions. An example of the latter is: almost all languages have at least one nasal consonant. Some universals are termed implicational or statistical. They usually take the form: 'If a language has X, it will have Y'. For example, if a language has inflections, e.g. the *-s* of *cats*, then it will have derivations, e.g. the *-ness* of *kindness.*

More recently other kinds of universals have been proposed. Linguist Anna Wierzbicka and her colleagues have found words for I, YOU, SOMEONE, SOMETHING, PEOPLE, THIS, THAT as well as many others in a sample of languages that statistically indicates their universality. They term these universal words semantic primitives (Wierzbicka: 1996). It is also claimed that the mechanisms of language change, such as those that lead to the grammaticization of certain lexical items, are also universal (Bybee et al. 1994). Another universal claimed for language is that they all, to some indefinable extent, rely on conventions to facilitate communication (Millikan 2005). Another significant universal concerns the acquisition of language: by and large, children learn language in the same stages and within the same time frame.

The standard generative argument against diversity is to postulate a **deep** and a **surface** structure. At the 'deep', or underlying level, it is suggested that the sentence structures of the world's languages are the same. At this 'deep' level, they are represented in an abstract way that governs the way they change when spoken at the 'surface' level. Variationists argue that this attempt to lessen the importance of variation is too abstract to verify and does not explain what is happening in the case of languages that have free word order.

Despite the discovery of a number of universals, the question as to whether languages have more similarities or differences remains unresolved. Linguist David Crystal puts it nicely when he asks, 'If two languages are 90 per cent similar in phonology and 50 per cent similar in grammar, are they more or less closely related than two languages which are 50 per cent similar in phonology and 90 per cent in grammar?' (Crystal 1997a: 296). Add to this the fact that languages are changing all the time and you have a mosaic: roughly 6,000 languages, some more, some less, some not at all alike, in flux, with some changing more rapidly than others. In short, extraordinary diversity.

Conclusion

The arbitrary nature of many aspects of language suggests that it is at the mercy of dynamic processes. These historical processes force changes to both culture and language. Their changes affect one another. Sometimes the changes will act upon the imbalances and imperfections within the system of language, sometimes upon the norms and values of the culture that the language and its use reflect. Some of the changes will be noticed, especially those that affect the sounds and meanings of words. Others, especially those that concern cultural attitudes, may go unnoticed because they are so slight or so great that they span generations. In this respect, language is like a ship. We witness only what is above the waves. The rest – the attitudes and values that underpin the culture it expresses – are below the surface, less visible, more difficult to grasp and only vaguely felt. And the whole, to continue the simile, appears to be flowing through time, its superstructure embedded in the lives of its speakers, and yet living longer than any individual. This is, truly, the vessel of history.

The reasons, both external and internal, that cause languages to change, live or die, are testament to the fact that languages depend for their natural survival in their spoken form not only upon the vitality of their culture, number of speakers and geographical distribution, but also to the extent that they can adapt to the intrusion of other languages and cultures. For languages teetering on the brink of extinction, this may mean relying upon the mercy of more powerful cultures.

Chapter 4: *We began by showing how action is orientated by norms and values and how this creates conventions that facilitate communication. We then looked at language from a cultural anthropological perspective. We saw that the influence of culture on language and the way we use it is all-pervasive. There is a dynamic interaction between the two. Despite numerous factors forcing language to change, its system remains relatively stable because of the slow pace and piecemeal nature of change. We looked at the different ways different languages express both similar and fundamental experiences. Latterly, we considered claims that all languages are fundamentally the same and concluded that the degree of similarity or differences between languages remains unresolved.*

Study Questions

1. Do you know of any similarities or differences between English and another language that you think stems from cultural reasons?
2. Thinking of differences between languages, do you think we can clearly differentiate between cultural and grammatical differences? What criteria would you choose for such a distinction?
3. Do you think languages that belong to the same family (such as English and German) have fewer cultural differences than those that belong to different families (such as French and Vietnamese)? Or, do you think they have as many differences, but are just less obvious? Give your reasons.
4. To what extent do you think language colours the way we see things?
5. Can you think of expressions that have attached themselves to particular social acts and become fixed? Offer some examples for discussion.

Chapter 5: *In the next chapter, we shall consider language in the context of linguistics, the scientific study of language.*

Where Does Noam Chomsky Fit into Linguistics?

Introduction

This question brings us to how the American linguist Noam Chomsky not only changed the direction and focus of linguistics but also challenged our way of thinking about language. Like everyone else, he has a past and emerged from a tradition. So the first thing we shall do is provide a bit of background. A brief history of linguistics prior to his arrival will provide the setting against which the changes he initiated can be understood. This done, his main ideas and contributions will be outlined. Not an easy task, since not only did he write prolifically over a period of 30-odd years, but his ideas were constantly developing. For the sake of brevity as well as ease of understanding, the spotlight will be on how linguistics changed. Latterly, we will summarize his legacy.

The Early Study of Language

It is hardly surprising that language was originally believed to be a gift from the gods that raised us from the lowly status of animals. This view is abundantly clear in the opening lines of *The Gospel of St. John*, 'In the beginning was the Word, and the Word was with God, and the Word was God.' Yet, despite the prevalence of religious views, language was studied in a secular and objective manner in the ancient civilizations of India, China and Greece. Naturally, it was its study in Greece that exerted most influence on the early direction of European interest because of its proximity.

According to linguist Ronald Wardhaugh, the Greeks were most interested in language's written forms and **rhetoric** (the arts of persuasion), an approach to language exemplified by the *Téchnē Grammatikē* written by Dionysius Thrax (1993: 2). The legacy of Greek civilization was inherited by scholars of the Roman Empire who began examining the structure of sentences. Two scholars in particular – Donatus and Priscian – analysed words into parts of speech, attributed different grammatical functions to them, and described types of phrases and clauses, showing how they combined in sentences. This method of study would dominate the teaching of language throughout Europe right up to the end of the twentieth century. The stubborn refusal of English, a Germanic language, to succumb neatly to an analysis intended for Latin would lead an educated, influential minority to describe it as an inferior tongue. From this view arose **prescriptivism**, a pedagogic type of grammar that describes the socially 'correct' use of language.

The escape from this classical agenda and its associated prescriptive approach into the realm of science took a very long time. It was not instigated by teachers, but by scholars of language. Their investigations would eventually shake off the mantle of classicism and make language study scientific.

Towards the Scientific Study of Language

Four dates are usually cited as most important in the movement towards the scientific study of language – 1786, 1875, 1916 and 1957. Let's begin with the first.

By 1700, the work of Pānini (*c*.500 BC) and other Indian linguists on Sanskrit had been discovered by European scholars. It was an independent tradition that was immediately recognized as superior, especially regarding phonetics. The study of that tradition culminated in Sir William Jones reading a paper to the *Royal Asiatic Society* in Calcutta in 1786. In that address, he showed how

Greek, Latin, Gothic, Celtic and Old Persian languages were related to Sanskrit. This dealt a death blow to the hitherto biblical explanation of linguistic diversity found in the Old Testament story of the Tower of Babel. It also provided an enormous impetus to historical and comparative research into language. As a result, the year 1786 is often viewed as a watershed dividing the scientific process of discovering data that fitted the facts of language from unscientific methods.

The momentum given to comparative research would continue right through the eighteenth and nineteenth centuries, all the time becoming more and more influenced by the methodology of the natural sciences. The stunning successes of the natural sciences – particularly physics, chemistry and biology – had attracted the attention of scholars in all fields of human enquiry. Linguists, too, began to adopt similar methods of experimentation and careful observation until, by the late nineteenth century, language study began to become more and more objective.

German-speaking scholars were at the forefront of this research movement that became known as **historical** or **comparative linguistics**. One of the earliest was Wilhelm von Humboldt (1767–1835). He wrote widely on language, stressing the innate ability of humankind for language and contrasting specific differences to universal features. Another was Friedrich Schlegel (1772–1829) who, in 1808, wrote a treatise on Sanskrit in which he urged scholars to search for the 'inner structures' that could prove connections between languages. Two scholars involved in the comparative and historical study of the Indo-European family of languages were the German Jacob Grimm (1785–1863) and the Dane Rasmus Rask (1787–1832). They began to uncover sound shifts that would eventually be formulated into sound laws. Franz Bopp (1791–1867) made a major contribution by tracing the development of inflected word forms from Sanskrit. August Schleicher (1821–68) introduced a biological approach to language study in his reconstruction and grammatical description of the **Proto** Indo-European language (an early stage of a language, or, in this case, a language family).

The work of these and other scholars culminated in the recognition of order underlying the formal features of the Indo-European languages. This realization led a group of German scholars called the *Junggrammatiker*, the neogrammarians, to propose a theory in 1875. It stated that, 'all sound changes occur under laws that allow no exceptions within the same dialect, so that the same sound, in the same environment, will always develop in the same fashion' (Fischer 1991: 161). It was the predictive nature of this sound law that put it squarely in the domain of science and, in retrospect, made 1875 the second most important milestone in the modern history of linguistics.

The neogrammarians – led by Karl Brugmann and Hermann Paul – then, somewhat unfairly, began to attack comparative linguistics as unsystematic until their movement, which was more concerned with living languages, replaced it as the new direction for research. Speculation was now put aside to address only data and the laws governing data. In effect, they had thrown down the gauntlet: if you did not accept their thesis that there was regularity in the sound changes of languages over time, then variation was random and scientific methods could not be applied. They were declaring that language study had to be scientific.

Not all scholars were enamoured with the disciplined approach of neogrammarian methodology, however. Ferdinand de Saussure (1857–1913) escaped their stronghold of Leipzig, then Paris, until he found the relative backwater of Geneva to give lectures on his very different view of language. After his death, his students compiled his lecture notes into a book entitled *Cours de linguistique générale.* Published in 1916, this slim book was hugely influential. It laid the foundations of a new movement of thought – **structuralism**. Structuralism viewed language as a closed system of elements and rules whose interactions accounted for the production and social communication of meaning. The influence of structuralism during the twentieth century was enormous, and this is why 1916 is cited as the third most important date in the modern history of linguistics. Gradually, it replaced comparative and historical approaches as the main paradigm. Through the fifties and seventies, it was dramatically developed to provide explanations for phenomena studied by other disciplines, such as anthropology and semiotics.

Saussure made several important distinctions concerning language study. The first was between **diachronic** and **synchronic** studies. The former referred to the historical study of language changes, the latter to its study at a particular, usually contemporary, point in time. The second was between *langue* (the system of language), *parole* (the actual use of language), and *faculté de langage* (general competence for the acquisition of language). Essentially, *langue* was a model for describing language that allowed researchers to screen out variables found in the use of language. Saussure stated that *langue* was to be studied synchronically within a system of lexical, grammatical and phonological elements all operating relative to each other. In other words, the focus was on the rules of language patterns with data drawn from *parole*. He also described the linguistic sign as **arbitrary** (not motivated by resemblance to the thing named). This means that **signs** (words) work not so much by referring to the things and events of the world, but by being a part of a system of signs. In this way, Saussure avoided the thorny question of meaning by describing its use as difference within a system of signs. The system created meaning by manipulating the differences between the signs. Saussure also stated that the sign has two aspects – a concept and an acoustic image.

One of the first to be influenced by Saussure's ideas was the leader of the Copenhagen Linguistic Circle, the Dane Louis Hjelmslev (1899–1965). He developed a theory of language as a social-semiotic called 'glossematics'. Next, was the Prague School headed by such personalities as Nicholas Trubetzkoy and Roman Jakobson. They applied structuralist ideas to phonology with groundbreaking results.

In the New World, linguistics was established by Franz Boas (1858–1942), Edward Sapir (1884–1939) and Leonard Bloomfield (1887–1949). They were all trained in neogrammarian linguistics, and Boas and Sapir were, in fact, German-born Americans. In time, a home-grown structuralism emerged that was very different to its European version.

Boas, using the techniques of descriptive linguistics to record native, American languages, made anthropology a fundamental part of linguistic study. His descriptions of cultures that had no script caused a shift away from the comparative approach of earlier linguists and eventually helped establish cultural anthropology as a separate discipline.

Inspired by Boas and strongly influenced by Wilhelm von Humboldt's linguistic theories, Sapir published widely on anthropological and linguistic issues. His central conviction was that language and culture were inseparable, a view encapsulated by the Sapir-Whorf Hypothesis mentioned in Chapter 4. Sapir was a relativist who saw no universal core to language, only languages. This was partly due to the fact that the presence of so many very different American Indian languages created an impression of the widest possible diversity. Although linguists were not showing much interest in semantics at that time, one tradition that grew out of the work of Sapir developed into a kind of structural-lexical semantics called **componential analysis** (a technique for representing the sense of lexemes). Later it would influence theories about semantic prototypes and primitives.

It is generally acknowledged that Bloomfield's influence was greater than even Boas's and Sapir's. He did more than anyone else to transform linguistics into a pursuit of science in America. He established the *Linguistic Society of America* and, by doing so, managed to separate linguistics from related disciplines such as literature, philology, anthropology and psychology. This gave it an independence and pride of position it did not have before. His work shunned the slippery question of meaning by arguing it was too vague, too mentalist, and that it was better to adopt the 'physicalist' approach of **behaviourist psychology**. This approach excluded all data that was not directly observable or physically measurable, such as speaker's intentions and contextual factors that could affect meaning. Although it seems odd that a branch of psychology could dismiss the unobservable happenings of the mind, at that time everyone wanted to be more scientific and one way to do this was to avoid abstract speculation. For Bloomfield, the useful thing about adopting this version of behaviourism was that it enabled him to push **semantics** (the study of meaning) to one side. His classic, *Language* (1933), became the leading university textbook on linguistics and began to influence the direction of the entire discipline. His main interest was grammar and, by applying Saussure's ideas on segmentation to the analysis of sentences, he began to lay the foundations for **phrase structure grammar**.

The aim of this new grammar was to describe the syntactic structure of sentences as a hierarchy of ordered **constituent** structures. Constituent was a technical term for linguistic units. For example, in the sentence 'The professor gives a lecture' each word is a constituent. The way to create a hierarchy was to join two or more constituents to form larger units. But they could only be joined if they became a simpler expression that belonged to some grammatical category. In the above example, 'the professor' can be replaced by 'he' or 'she' and 'gives a lecture' by 'teaches'. So this sentence's hierarchy could be represented by a **tree diagram** as in Figure 10.

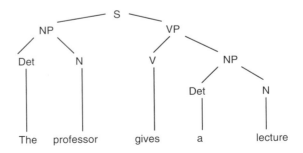

Figure 10 Tree diagram 1

In this tree diagram, NP (noun phrase) and VP (verb phrase) are called immediate constituents of S (sentence), while Det (determiner) and N (noun) are immediate constituents of NP, and so on. This method of analysis was called **Immediate Constituent analysis** (IC analysis).

After his death in 1949, the 'post-Bloomfieldian era' continued into the 1950s. Most American linguists focussed their studies on formal analysis in which the phoneme and morpheme took centre stage. But IC analysis continued to be applied to sentences using tree diagrams and phrase structure rules. Bloomfield's successors – Bernard Bloch, George Trager, Charles Hockett and Zellig Harris among others – continued to develop his methodology. Zellig Harris, Chomsky's teacher, worked at expanding the scope of IC analysis into syntax where it was weakest.

The first real challenge to Bloomfieldian structuralism came from the London School in the 1950s. There, J. R. Firth (1890–1960) disliked the atomistic approach of Bloomfieldians, the way they reduced language to its smallest components. Drawing upon the work of anthropologists such as Malinowski, he developed a theory of 'context of situation'. In this theory, meanings were referred to their various functions in particular contexts. Like Saussure, Firth never committed his ideas to paper. This was left to his most able student – Michael Halliday. Halliday set himself the task of giving a full account of Firth's theory which, after various names, finally came to be known as **systemic grammar**. But this early challenge would be overshadowed by developments on American soil.

By the 1950s, the idea that only the scientific study of language could warrant respect had firmly established itself. It was then, as if right on cue, a very scientific kind of linguist appeared in the wings waiting to make his entrance. His name was Noam Chomsky. His background was philosophy, logic and mathematics – an unusual combination and one which would produce a kind of mathematical linguistics that some would love and others hate.

A New Grammar is Born

The fourth most important date in the history of modern linguistics is 1957. It was the year in which Chomsky's *Syntactic Structures* was published. This slim book brought his theoretical investigations to the notice of a wider public. It was based upon a much larger work, his then unpublished doctoral thesis, the *Logical Structure of Linguistic Theory*. In these works, he defines an ascending scale of types of grammars. Very briefly, his proposal was that a grammar was 'a device that generates all of the grammatical sequences' and none of the ungrammatical ones (Chomsky 1957: 13). This 'all-and-only' principle was the litmus test of the worth, or explanatory power, of a grammar. He argued that **surface sentence** structures (the directly observable form of sentences, as they are spoken) were generated (in the mathematical sense of 'converted') by the transformational rules of a phrase structure grammar. This new grammar was called **transformational-generative grammar** (T-G grammar for short).

Phrase structure grammar was not Chomsky's creation, it was inherited from American structuralists. They, however, had only used it to analyse syntax at surface structure level. Chomsky added transformational rules to it because it could not explain certain syntactic–semantic problems. For example, in the sentence *Philip called his brother up* phrase structure grammar was unable to explain the way 'up' is placed in relation to the verb. It could come after 'called' or after 'brother'. Another problem it seemed unable to resolve were cases of ambiguity. For example, in the phrase *the discovery of the student,* it is not clear if the student has discovered something or whether s/he has been found. Nor could the rules of phrase structure grammar explain the relation between active–passive sentences of the sort 'Tom hit Mary' and 'Mary was hit by Tom' that seem to be related. These and other difficulties prompted Chomsky to propose transformational rules. It was quickly recognized that these additional rules helped phrase structure grammar to explain more with greater economy and consistency.

When *Syntactic Structures* first appeared Bloomfieldians welcomed it as an extension of their phrase structure grammar, as they did Zellig Harris's earlier address to the *Linguistic Society of America* on 'Transformations in Linguistic Structures'. They did not immediately grasp that it would undermine the entire orientation of their approach to language description. Hitherto, they had only analysed the observable facts of sentences, moving along its elements in a linear fashion from left to right. They did not see that Chomsky had introduced an underground spring, one that could appeal to hidden mental processes of conversion which would radically change how the distributional facts of a sentence could be explained.

When Chomsky's scathing review of B. F. Skinner's *Verbal Behaviour* appeared in 1959, Bloomfieldians realized the full implications of his ideas. Skinner was the high priest of behaviourist psychology and Chomsky was attacking his ideas, the very ideas that formed the philosophical foundations of their beliefs regarding language. Academics began to take sides, and two camps formed on either side of an intellectual divide. Dialogue across that divide became increasingly difficult as insults were traded. Not everyone in linguistics was involved because not everyone was interested in theory, but theory is the high ground, and Chomsky and his cadres began the fight to take it.

New Foundations

During the 1960s, the focus of linguistic study began to change more rapidly as Chomsky developed his **innateness hypothesis**. The hypothesis was that children are born knowing what human languages are like and, because they possess this blueprint, they will acquire perfectly whatever language they are exposed to. It was a view totally opposed to behaviourist theories that argue the links between language learning and society. Innateness was the reason given for thinking that a Universal Grammar (hereafter UG) might exist in the human mind in some genetic form.

Innateness was not an original idea: it has its roots in the theories of the Latin Grammarians, Wilhelm von Humboldt and the seventeenth-century Port Royal grammarians of Versailles. Chomsky readily acknowledged these sources as his inspiration and described his linguistics as 'Cartesian' after the French philosopher Descartes. He particularly shared Descartes' beliefs on 'innate ideas' and 'innate principles' that have no connection to experience.

In retrospect, we can see that Skinner's behaviourist account of language was too 'mechanistic'. Drawing its findings from laboratory experiments on animals, it was too **reductionist**; that is, it reduced the explanation of language use to a mere 'nothing but' responses to stimuli. It was a view that Chomsky found totally unacceptable. By excluding all unobservable behaviour and making exaggerated claims, Skinner had left himself open to attack. But what of other behaviourist accounts? Did Chomsky find these more acceptable? Not at all. The reasons will become clearer as we continue, but, basically, Chomsky's attacks on all forms of behaviourism signalled the beginning of a long march for a new generation of linguists. It would take them away from language's connections to society towards the role of a mental grammar.

In a relatively short time, the battle for the high ground was over. T-G grammar ruled and descriptive grammars were now derogatively dismissed as 'traditional' and inadequate. Chomsky spelt out two levels of 'adequacy' for a grammar – descriptive and explanatory. A grammar is descriptive if it enables a proper description of a language to be made. It is explanatory only if it explains the form of that description and the means by which the child's first language is apparently effortlessly acquired. Most grammars rarely satisfied the first and were not usually concerned with the second.

Chomsky continued to argue that a number of important characteristics of language are built into our brains as part of our genetic endowment (the **language faculty**) and distinct from our general cognitive intelligence. This argument rested on the observation that language appeared to operate independently of our visual, artistic, musical, logical and mathematical abilities. You will recall that in Chapter 3 this view of the structure of the mind was termed modular. It claims that language is acquired, rather than learnt, and that it is merely a matter of sorting out the details because the universal properties are already present from birth in the language module.

The innateness hypothesis was controversial from the outset and has remained so because it is extremely difficult to prove that language is separate from our general intelligence and that, somewhere in the brain, there is a distinct language-generating mechanism. Critics argued that language is part and parcel of our general cognitive abilities. Chomsky and his supporters answered such objections in a number of ways: first, by attempting to identify universal properties of language in order to formulate the principles of UG; second, by pointing out how few errors children make when acquiring a language, and how certain errors (which one would expect them to make) are never made; and third, they claim children could never deduce all the rules of language, the data is inadequate to the knowledge. The third point is known as the **poverty of the stimulus** argument, the same used against Skinner.

From a Theory of Grammar to a Theory of Language

Gradually, T-G grammar proved too much of a mouthful and gave way to the smoothly alliterative **generative grammar**. The latter began to expand into a general theory of language that included phonology and semantics. This was called the 'aspects model' or 'standard theory' after its source – Chomsky's *Aspects of the Theory of Syntax* (1965). Its phonological aspect owed a great deal to Chomsky's long-standing collaboration with Morris Halle. They co-authored *The Sound Pattern of English* (1968) to replace Bloomfieldian phonology with a generative phonology. The semantic component was the work of Jerrold Katz and Jerry Fodor. They were the first to place a semantic theory within the generative framework.

The concept of **deep structure** (an abstract level from which rules generated sentence transformations) was introduced. The notion of deep structure has undergone many revisions and was eventually discarded in favour of language faculty. Here we shall refer to what is generally described as its classical version using Figure 11.

This Figure shows that the deep structure of a sentence is the output of the base component to both the transformational component and the semantic component. The surface structure of a sentence is the output of the transformational component to

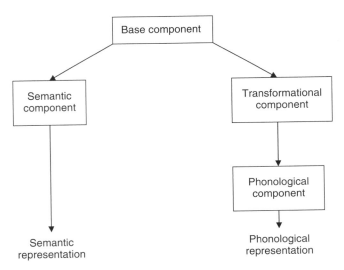

Figure 11 The standard theory's notion of deep structure

the phonological component which becomes surface structure if represented phonologically.

The theory expressed the famous, or notorious, depending on your point of view, principle that transformations do not affect meaning. In the Figure, there is no arrow leading from the transformational component to the semantic component. Just like Saussure and Bloomfield, Chomsky wanted to push semantics to one side; here, he does this by separating the semantic roles of lexicon and syntax. The base component conveniently contained not only the non-transformational categorical rules of syntax for the language in question, but also its lexicon, or dictionary. The lexicon provides all the syntactic, semantic and phonological rules for every lexeme in the language.

At first, this theory was hailed as the first to link sound to meaning via syntax. The details were not clear, but euphoria reigned. Gradually, it evaporated and criticism became more and more vociferous. Most of it was directed at its semantic component. Had Chomsky's theory, like Skinner's, over-extended itself? Critics argued that the semantic aspect was inadequate and that the semantic interpretation of a sentence depends on surface structure phenomena such as intonation, word order and extra-linguistic factors such as context. Arguments for and against the notion of deep structure and a whole range of other issues led to a split in the generative movement from which two competing approaches emerged – generative semantics and, later, a slightly more Chomskyan version, called General Phrase Structure Grammar. The former was led by Lakoff, McCawley and Ross, the latter by Gazdar.

Reacting to criticism, standard theory was developed into **extended standard theory**, and then revised by Jackendoff and Chomsky to become **Revised Extended Standard Theory** in 1972, but, eventually, monopoly rights on a standard theory had to be relinquished. There were now too many generative grammars.

About this time the number of transformation rules in Chomsky's generative grammar began to mushroom out of control and a concerted effort was made to reduce, not just their number, but also their role. What had once been described as transformations were now marked as abstract elements in a deep structure that triggered particular surface representations. Gradually, this process of reduction led to just one transformational rule, *move alpha*. This meant move what can be moved within the limits prescribed by the rest of the system. This reflected a new focus on research: how far could certain words in a sentence be moved away from others that they were dependent upon for their meaning. For example, in the following, 'On our answer to this question must depend the validity of the whole of our experiences as to the future,' is the 'On' placed too far from 'depend'? Could it be separated any further or would that sunder their semantic link?

Since the seventies there have been at least two more significant developments – **Theory of Government and Binding** and, latterly, a **Minimalist Program.** Very briefly, government deals with the assignment of specific grammatical roles to words and word groups. Binding refers to the conditions under which pronouns and some other words are or are not co-referentially interpreted. The minimalist program came about as the result of a search for a compact model, one that would state exactly what should be included among the various insights gained over the years concerning constituency, movement, government and binding.

It would be impossible to explain the details of each development in the space of one chapter, so, instead, we will look at examples that give a flavour of the generative method of sentence analysis. First, let's go back to the beginning and look at how transformational rules changed the tree diagrams of phrase structure grammar.

Tree Diagrams

You will recall that generativists were trying to disprove the variationist account of language because they believed there must be a basic underlying uniformity to language by the mere fact that all its users were human. Naturally, they thought that language universals might provide some clues that would lead to the principles of UG. One of the first to be adopted was the fact that all languages have nouns and verbs. This could be used to analyse all sentences into noun and verb phrases. This was expressed as in Figure 12.

Figure 13 shows a sentence subdivided below the level of NP and VP.

Linguist Ray Jackendoff writes that this notation was similar to the tree diagrams of phrase structure grammar insofar as it breaks a sentence into parts, but different in the way it labels each part as belonging to particular syntactic categories such as N, VP, etc.

On the usefulness of tree diagrams, Jackendoff writes that many variations in word order among the languages of the world become transparent when viewed in tree diagrams (1994: 71). Here's an example he offers in Figure 14 of English and French word order in which A stands for 'adjective'.

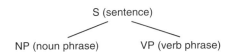

Figure 12 Tree diagram 2

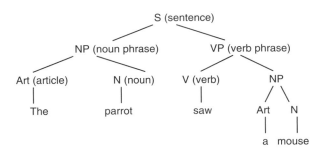

Figure 13 Tree diagram 3

Figure 14 Tree diagram 4

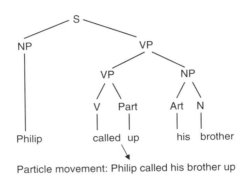

Particle movement: Philip called his brother up

Figure 15 Tree diagram 5

Presumably, Jackendoff's point is that, regardless of surface word order differences, at a deep level they are both noun phrases.

He argues that tree diagrams are useful for a number of other purposes, too. They can show how long, complex sentences are built up from a collection of simple patterns, provide a nice way of showing how some sentences can be disambiguated, and describe, though not explain, the movement of small elements in a sentence. Figure 15 'explains' an ambiguity mentioned earlier.

Tree diagrams can also be used to illustrate another aspect of language – **recursion.** In some sentences you can get noun phrases within noun phrases, or sentences embedded within sentences that illustrate the same pattern and the same repeated use of a rule. For example, in this children's ditty, *This is the dog that chased the cat that killed the rat,* it is clear that whatever rule yields *that*

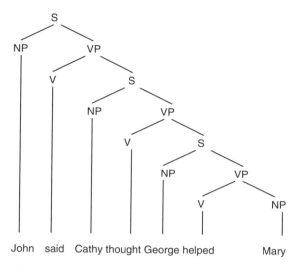

Figure 16 Tree diagram 6

chased the cat must be reapplied to get *that killed the rat*. This is known as recursion. Figure 16 shows how tree diagrams illustrate recursive rules.

It seems odd that despite this reiteration generativists still feel justified in claiming that most sentences we speak and hear are new and creative.

Syntactic Movement

Syntactic movement is another area that Chomsky and other generativists are very interested in. Chomsky has called the way phrases are interpreted as if they were in a different position in a sentence the 'displacement property' of language. It has led others to investigate phrase movement in sentences in a number of language studies. An example from English is:

Who do [you think [that John believes [that Mary said [that Tom saw]]]]?

The square brackets represent the boundaries of relative clauses. In this example, the word 'who' has moved to the front of the sentence from the object position after 'saw'. Biolinguist Lyle Jenkins writes that the real question for researchers in language design here is, 'does *who* move in one fell swoop to the beginning of the sentence or does it move step-wise to the front?' (2000: 146). Although the evidence is not yet conclusive, he suggests that the step-wise hypothesis that Chomsky originally proposed may be true, but also, and more importantly, that it is research into questions like these that will eventually uncover the internal workings of language.

It should be clear from these examples that generative linguists are overwhelmingly interested in syntax. Grammar was so important to them that a new model of language was proposed. Let's compare it to the standard model to see the difference.

Old and New Models

Probably, the most common model of language found in introductory textbooks to linguistics is the one shown in Figure 17.

From this model, we can see that four basic levels are attributed to language's structure – meaning, grammar, phonetics and phonology. Morphology is usually subsumed within grammar and **pragmatics** (study of meaning of utterances in situation) within semantics.

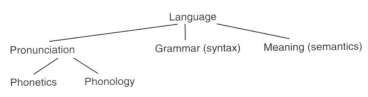

Figure 17 Four-level model of language structure

Figure 18 Three-level generative model of language structure

During the sixties and seventies, generativists argued for a deep mental grammar to embrace all aspects of language – phonology (sound patterns), syntax (sentence patterns) and semantics (meaning patterns). This model is shown in Figure 18.

Gradually, different models with different emphases began to appear within the various offshoots of the generative movement. Now there are many models to choose from. The aim today is to show how the various levels are integrated. Jackendoff models this integration as a flow of information (1994: 42). Speech production begins with a thought which is first structured syntactically, then phonologically, and lastly spoken. He omits thought and the final motor instructions for speech from his definition of language. For him, and most other generativists, language is syntactic and phonological structuring only. Speech perception flows in the opposite direction: auditory patterns enter the brain through our ears, the phonological structure is decoded, the syntactic structure next, and finally the thought is understood.

The Generative Movement Today

The split in the generative movement spawned various versions of generative grammars, some more, some less Chomskyan. The best-known formalist offshoots are **Categorial Grammar** and Gazdar's **Generalized Phrase Structure Grammar** (GPSG for short). Categorial grammar was first developed by Polish logicians and then applied to natural languages by linguists of a logical-mathematical turn of mind. The less Chomskyan versions drew their inspiration from the ideas of a logician, Richard Montague (1930–1971). Linguists who adopted and developed his ideas called it **Montague Grammar**. These grammars are equally generative but dispense with deep levels and transformations. According to Bussman, the grammars that developed out of categorial grammars 'have a semantically motivated formal syntax' (1996: 67). Gazdar's GPSG grew out of opposition to Chomsky's Revised Extended Standard Theory. It has no transformations and meanings are shown using the intensional logic of Montague Grammar. Bussman writes that GPSG belongs to a family of unification grammars that link semantics to syntax (1996: 182). In general, these grammars are not interested in providing philosophical foundations, but in creating models that can form the basis for computer programs for language processing and translation.

Chomsky's philosophical argument for innateness stimulated research in two branches of linguistics – cognitive linguistics and biolinguistics. It was also instrumental in helping the establishment of an interdisciplinary enterprise called **cognitive science**. The latter approaches the question of how we understand language from a broader spectrum of general cognitive abilities than cognitive linguistics which attempts to limit its approach to questions of language design. These cognitive approaches ousted former behaviourist ones. The best-known exponents of cognitive linguistics are Lakoff, Talmy and Fauconnier, and an important offshoot is **Cognitive Grammar** established by Ronald Langacker in the 1980s. It views syntax as inherently symbolic and much more closely related to other mental activities.

There are now so many different systems of generative grammar other than Chomsky's that semanticist Sir John Lyons writes, 'No one of these enjoys supremacy' and that no linguist would think there is a straight choice between two rival systems of linguistic analysis and description when it comes to the integration of semantics and syntax (1995: 223). Just how well these grammars integrate semantics is open to debate and a point that will be taken up in a later chapter. With generative grammars enjoying the limelight, it is easy to forget that there are other kinds on offer. The most common are **descriptive grammars**, such as Quirk et al.'s for English (1985). These describe the more obvious rules of a language. There are also functional grammars and a host of other less well-known ones that still serve useful purposes.

The Legacy

Now that some of the furore that surrounded the generative movement has died down, it is becoming possible to assess the situation. There is no doubt that the generative paradigm has established itself. Its orientation is structural, but it adds to previous Saussurean notions of system by claiming that the rules and representations of grammar are in the mind-brain (a Chomskyan term) and innately so. It has taken the study of syntax much further than previous efforts and promoted it to such an extent that Norbert Hornstein, in his introduction to the second edition of Chomsky's *Rules and Representations*, writes that we can no longer say linguistics is the study of language (2005: xxxiii). Its new focus is the study of the language faculty. For those who agree with him, linguistics is no longer one of the humanities, but a mental science studying the structures of mind-brain states. A fact that suggests the title of this chapter should be revised.

At the time of writing, Chomsky was 79 and, naturally, not as involved in linguistics as he was. He has passed the baton onto younger generations. But, for the 30-odd years he was at the helm, he faced criticism head on and, not only did he hold his corner, but with the help of other leading intellectuals, built up a strong philosophical position. Of one thing there can be no doubt, he became a leading thinker of our time. As his legacy we can cite the following. He has

(i) shown what criteria formal theories of grammar should meet;

(ii) laid the foundations and pointed the directions for constructing the most powerful formal grammars to date;

(iii) maintained that a grammar characterizes an internal structure of logical formulations (rules) for organizing linguistic representations;

(iv) reintroduced the contention that language is innate and not derived solely from processes of socialization;

(v) strengthened the formalist contention that syntax is the essence of language, a self-contained system at its core;

(vi) limited the scope of linguistic enquiry by giving priority to research findings that can be formulated and so, in his definition, termed scientific;

(vii) stimulated research in cognitive linguistics, biolinguistics, cognitive science, philosophy of language, philosophy of mind and neuroscience;

(viii) significantly raised the status of linguistics and the level of debate across a number of related fields;

(ix) made theoretical linguistics a branch of psychology by directing research towards revealing what the workings of language tell us about the mind; and

(x) shifted the philosophical underpinning of mainstream linguistics from the empirical approach of behaviourism to the rationalist approach of emphasizing the role of the mind.

The fact that Chomsky's ideas have been able to branch out in so many directions, assuming the forms of various generative grammars, shows that the generative thesis has benefited formal descriptions of language. The philosophical grounding that Chomsky proposed for the generative model has not had the same degree of success because of the strong claims made for innateness. If evidence for the genetic base claimed for language is not forthcoming, then attention may swing back to language's connections to learning and experience or other explanations. Although opinions are still divided over some issues that Chomsky has raised, generative theory has had such a profound influence upon the direction and purpose of linguistic enquiry that, like it or not, you cannot ignore it. It has set the agenda for linguistics during the second half of the twentieth century.

Conclusion

One outcome of the Chomskyan era has been a split within the linguistic community. This has been accomplished by elevating the importance of grammar and devaluing the work of sociolinguists and others describing how language is actually used. It seems as if Chomskyan formalists either want to separate themselves from the rest of the linguistic community or believe that their specialization is forcing them to part company. Robins, a historian of linguistics, writes that general linguistics is no longer a unified discipline and, 'the days of a general introduction to the whole subject by a single author may be numbered' (1997: 269–270). Since one reason for this rift is the claim by formalists that their approach is more scientific, the next chapter will consider what is scientific.

Chapter 5: We described how the study of language was gradually drawn under the aegis of science, how various movements of thought – historical, comparative, biological – eventually gave way to Saussure's structuralism. In America, a very atomistic form of structuralism developed under the direction and inspiration of Bloomfield. After his death, the scene was set for advances in syntax and a young Noam Chomsky had the idea that would set alight the imagination of a new generation of linguists. There is no doubt that generative grammar has been the most influential theory of the latter half of the twentieth century, but the price of that success has been to cleave the linguistic community apart. It has so changed the direction of theoretical linguistic enquiry that, ironically, it may be sounding the death knell of linguistics by declaring it a mental science, a branch of cognitive psychology.

Study Questions

1. Find out what you can about the sound laws that the neogrammarians claimed to have uncovered.
2. Find out what language universals Greenberg discovered in his survey and classify them according to type.
3. How should we decide whether languages are similar or different?
4. How real do you think the formal models of language that grammarians create are? Do they correspond to the facts? Or are they the best explanations to date?

Chapter 6: In the next chapter, we will consider what scientific criteria linguistic theories are supposed to meet.

How Scientific can Linguistic Theory Be?

Introduction

Chomsky denies that a clear concept of language as a public phenomenon is possible: 'a notion of "common, public language" that remains mysterious ... useless for any form of theoretical explanation ... There is simply no way of making sense of this prong of the externalist theory of meaning and language' (Chomsky qtd. in Millikan 2005: 24). This leads him to reject theories that analyse language in terms of how it is used in society by people – **externalist** or functionalist theories. He believes only a competence model will provide a viable means towards a scientific description.

Naturally, this criticism begs a definition of science. So we shall begin this chapter with an outline of the main features of scientific enquiry. This will be useful because we shall see what criteria linguistic theory is meant to meet. Next, we shall compare two theories, one formal and one functional, with regard to these features and ask if Chomsky's criticism is warranted.

The Scientific Approach

The hallmark of science is that it seeks to explain the natural world in terms of nature. Because it makes claims that it maintains are truer than other explanations about the way things are in the world, its assumptions are of great interest to philosophers. So important, in fact, that **philosophy of science** constitutes a branch of philosophy. Its account of science may not exactly match what scientists do, but it is about the truth of science's claims. Since the brunt of Chomsky's criticism is that externalist theories are not as scientific as formal or **internalist** theories, we shall begin by listing the main features that ground science's claims to truth.

The Hypothesis and Testing

Every serious researcher has an idea about his or her research, and when that idea is shaped into a hypothesis it forms the research question. The idea behind the research question may have come from examining data or even from a dream. The source scarcely matters. Nor does it matter if the researcher fervently believes the hypothesis to be true, because believing is not knowing. Much more important is that it can be systematically checked. In other words, the hypothesis should be testable. For example, linguists ask: How do words combine in sentences to form meaningful utterances? What are the basic units of language? How do children acquire language? How do languages vary and change over time? Why do they change and vary? What criteria should be chosen to classify them? Do all languages share certain characteristics?

The testing is usually done against a statistically representative sample of relevant data, or by experiment, careful observation or a combination of methods. Testing is an attempt to measure so as to gauge differences. Measurement, or quantification, places the object of enquiry in a neutral, mathematical, light.

Findings are usually explained in the framework of existing theory. But if results run counter to theory, then the researcher might suggest an adjustment, or, in rarer cases, an entirely new theory. In this, we see feedback between theory and results: new findings can change theory and new theory can change the way data is regarded.

Today, answered means supported by evidence. Evidence allows others to follow the same procedures to verify or refute what has been claimed. In this way, knowledge is placed in the public domain.

When theories can neither be proved nor disproved, no one is ever very happy. The aim is to keep everything as objective as possible. The methods of science are designed to filter out subjectivity and offer a neutral unbiased view.

The Nature of the Data

Linguistics has a strong empirical basis because its data – the sounds and written symbols of language – are observable, i.e. susceptible to the senses. However, it is rare in the social sciences and humanities to find research that is entirely empirical. With the exception of the sounds of language, much linguistic data is unlike that of the physical sciences because it is not easily reduced to basic units that are self-evident. Are the smallest units of meaning (morphemes) the basic units, or words, or sentences that capture a complete thought?

The data of language is also too varied to handle in its entirety. Decisions have to be made about how much and what kind of data should be selected for investigation. This is one of the reasons why the study of language has been divided into models of competence/performance or *langue/parole*. Such distinctions enable researchers to limit the data under consideration, thereby decreasing the number of variables and gaining more control over the data. Formal descriptions, by virtue of their very nature, exclude the variation found in language.

Controlling the data can, however, skew results. It has been claimed that using a model of language idealizes linguistic data and thereby introduces a bias. Yet, in the scientific community, limiting the data is considered legitimate practice, as long as there is not too much 'explaining away' of awkward data. It amounts to a trade-off between rigour and comprehensiveness. By limiting the data you obtain greater rigour, but it is at the expense of the explanation which becomes narrower and less comprehensive.

Methodology

Because the methods chosen for an investigation are determined by the nature of the enquiry, we shall look at a specific example. You will recall that in Chomsky's case, the aim was to study the fine structure of the faculty of language (FL). Now how does one probe part of the brain? Look inward and reflect upon what your mind is doing? Right from the outset, Chomsky rejected both introspection and reflection as methods because he believed the rules were beyond the reach of consciousness (1980: 231). Instead, he proposed that, first, data should be selected that might reveal something interesting about the operation of rules upon sentence structure. Next, prepare the data, present it to native speakers, then let them decide intuitively which sentence among the sample is grammatical. This method has been dubbed 'black-box reasoning'. Here is an example:

1. Compare the acceptability of (a) and (b). Are they on a par, or is one better than the other?
   (a) I said that the women like each other.
   (b) The women said that I like each other.

We can see in this example that both negative and positive data are presented. This example is pretty straightforward and English speakers would invariably rank 1a over 1b, but Chomsky says there are cases when they cannot decide (1980: 120). Some believe that this method provides a window into FL.

The next step is to use the findings to figure out what rules or principles may lie behind the judgements of native speakers. Their decisions may be right, but they do not amount to an understanding. Once linguists are satisfied that they have adduced the rules, the last step is to ask how these rules have been acquired. This is claimed to be an exploration of the general structure of the language faculty.

Naturally, if the enquiry were concerned with other aspects of language, for example, spelling reform, or the teaching of spelling to young children, then completely different methods would be used. In this, we see that methods are chosen, just like tools, specifically for the task at hand. This highlights the intricate relationship between method, data and evidence. They form an iron triangle in which the object of enquiry affects not just methodology but even what counts as data and evidence.

Theory

As our understanding of the world develops, new questions arise and old ones are revised or rejected. This reinterpretation of data and construction of new theories is not like a merry-go-round, no better than the necessarily self-defeating cycles of the fashion world. They are an advance – witness the progress in transportation, medicine, computers, telecommunications, etc. But one may wonder how it is that theories that have been accepted as 'correct' for a very long time are suddenly overturned and proven wrong. How do we know that present theories are not wrong? The answer is we don't, it is just that we think they provide a better description of the facts than earlier ones. Science, just like every other human activity, has a history and is evolving through contact with other developments.

The kind of theory science likes best are those that have a predictive power that enable generalization. One of the best examples is the atomic theory of matter. It explains how big systems are made up of little systems and how changes in the behaviour of the little systems can cause changes to the behaviour of the big systems. The theory is concise, coherent, has explanatory power (because it explains most of the data), and its generalizations are predictive. In a similar way, a theory of language should say something that is true, not just about one language, but all languages.

A theory can, however, limit itself to one aspect of a phenomenon. For example, a theory of grammar may not explain everything about language, but it should at least explain what it defines as grammatical about language.

Different Views on Knowledge

Empiricism and rationalism form two different perspectives regarding knowledge. Let's consider each in turn.

The English philosopher John Locke (1632–1704) is generally recognized as the founder of modern **empiricism**, a school of thought which insists that knowledge must have its roots in experience, particularly the experience we derive from our senses. Strong forms of empiricism would like every claim to knowledge put to the test of experience. For science, that 'test of experience' is usually verification by experiment. The strength of experience as grounds for knowledge lies in the fact that it is based in the observable. If someone doesn't believe you, you can say, 'I'll show you.' In other words, observation allows others to witness, and so places the object of enquiry outside of individual subjectivity. The American philosopher W. v. Quine (1908–2000) described observation as 'the tribunal of science', and remarked that once you depart it you are on the road to theorizing (1970: 34).

If one imagines a spectrum at one end of which there is an example of research that yields results which have been tested against observable data with supporting theory that makes predictions that are also capable of being tested for their truth or falseness, then this kind of science is empirical. It deals with the observable, testable data of the natural world. It is 'hard' science. At the other end of the spectrum are questions and explanations that may not be testable, their theories may explain, but offer little proof. They may still be counted as science, however, because the underlying reasoning is logical. They may offer the best explanations to date for phenomena that are unobservable or do not lend themselves easily to testing. The claims of this kind of knowledge belong to **rationalism**.

Rationalism doubts knowledge that is drawn from experience because it comes from our unreliable senses. For this reason, there is a tension between rationalism and empiricism as to the scope and limitation of science. Rationalists believe experience can only show the appearance of the world, not the reality. The reality, they argue, can only be gained by rational reflection based upon self-evident principles. However, among such principles, some are recognized as more self-evident than others (Russell 1912: 68).

The difference between the two approaches is, in practice, often more one of emphasis than complete contrast. Usually adherents of both sides exhibit more of one tendency than another. The American philosopher William James (1842–1910) summarized their differences as follows:

Rationalism tends to emphasize universals and to make wholes prior to part in the order of logic as well as in that of being. Empiricism, on the contrary, lays the explanatory stress upon the part, the element, the individual, and treats the whole as a collection and the universal as an abstraction (1912: 22).

Both approaches have their weaknesses: empiricists can become obsessed with proof and rationalists carried away by abstract speculations.

Reasoning

The nature of scientific reasoning is different to that of many other activities. Scientists arrive at their beliefs by a process of inference that can be either **inductive** or **deductive**. The distinction between these two words is not always clear, but, generally speaking, empiricists tend to use the former, rationalists the latter. Deduction is said to proceed from the general to the general, or from the general to the particular. Induction moves from the particular to the particular, or from the particular to the general. Here's an example from Robins writing about Bloomfield's attitude towards Universal Grammar (UG). For Bloomfield UG 'was a potential product of long-term induction from great numbers of linguistic descriptions; the Chomskyans see it as a deductive working hypothesis' (1997: 267). In other words, whereas Bloomfieldians would examine the details of a language and induce to the possible existence of UG, Chomskyans begin with UG as a working hypothesis and deduce evidence from selected data to support the claim. Both words mean 'to draw inferences', but the starting point and direction of enquiry regarding the particular and the general differs.

Mathematics

Mathematics may seem far removed from questions of language, but the bridge that connects them is logic. In modern times, many philosophers have tried to demystify mathematics by showing that it is not a 'pure' form of knowledge that transcends human experience. One way to do this is to reduce it to logic and show its natural connections to language. For example, the German philosopher David Hilbert (1862–1943) treated mathematics as a formal language made up of a vocabulary and syntax. He demonstrated how recursive rules could explain the manner of their manipulation. Thus, we arrive at $1 + 1 + 1$ from $1 + 1$. The plus sign means exactly the same as the logical connector 'and' in a sentence such as, 'We need bananas and yogurt and honey,' etc. The reader will recall that this continued reapplication of a rule is called recursion. Later, Chomsky would argue that a few simple rules like these would allow us to construct an infinite number of sentences.

Formalists like to reduce the rules and operations of their descriptions to mathematical notations. They believe this reduction has a kind of Spartan elegance that reveals the essence behind the appearance. So, for example, 'NP + VP' is a formal expression of the sentence, 'The cat sat on the mat' (Noun Phrase followed by Verb Phrase).

Laws, Principles, Rules and Theory

The terms general law, law, principle, rule and theory are very frequent in academic literature and the differences in their meanings are not always clear. *The Encyclopaedia of Philosophy* gives laws precedence over theory because their terms refer to observable phenomena that are operationally definable and experimental (Edwards 1967: 404–410). Theory, on the other hand, may contain some terms that do not refer to observable phenomena and which may be difficult to identify, for example, the microscopic properties of quantum mechanics. In other words, the incontrovertibly real takes precedence over the assumed existence of non-observable or abstract entities in the value hierarchy of science.

In general, facts are described by laws, laws are explained by theory. Whilst laws are limited to description, theory adds an explanation. General laws are sometimes called 'laws of nature'. These are the most fundamental because they describe phenomena that cannot do otherwise – for example, the motions of the planets, or how, given gravity, water runs downhill, etc. Sometimes a theory can be a statement about a general principle rather than a law. But, even so, it must still base its claims about this principle on reasoned argument and offer evidence to explain particular facts. A principle lies halfway between a law and a general rule. It often seems to denote a general rule that lacks the degree of supporting evidence required of a law, but which is still important. It seems higher up on the ladder of truth than rule because it has greater generality, but lower than law because it does not meet the same required criteria for verification or have the same power to predict.

As the degree of supporting evidence decreases, so we move down the value hierarchy of science: from general law, to law, to general principle, to principle, to rule. And as evidence decreases, so, too, does the power of the theory to generalize and predict.

Summary

The above are the main features of scientific enquiry. They are set out in some detail because many of the problems faced by linguistic theory are directly related to how well it can explain language in terms of scientific belief. Before examining Chomsky's claim that externalist theories are unscientific, let's first look at some of the problems facing those brave individuals who take up the challenge of constructing a theory of language.

General Problems for Theorists

The first problem facing theorists is the point of entry. Starting points concern the level of description. The six levels that language has been divided into are shown in Figure 19.

Ranks	Levels	Units
Sound: vowel, consonant.	phonology	phonemes
Word: stem, prefix, suffix.	morphology	morphemes
Word: fixed phrase.	lexicon	lexemes
Sentence: word, phrase, clause.	syntax	syntagmemes
Meaning: predicate, argument.	semantics	sememes
Utterance: speech act, text, discourse	pragmatics	utteremes

Figure 19   Ranks, levels and units

The choice of level can influence the theory. For example, if pragmatics is chosen, the theory is likely to be functionalist; if syntax, then it is likely to be formalist. The choice of level will also influence the degree of rigour obtained in the theory; that is, how well the results can be formulated.

To date, the attempt to locate reality (that is, self-evident units) in language has been most successful in phonology. Theorists have tried to project the same methods and conceptions of phonology onto the other levels. But they have found that in the levels 'above' morphology there are no fully reliable criteria for defining units, each unit of a sequence differs from those before, or after it, in diverse and complex ways. Put simply, it becomes difficult to define the working unit. When this happens, theorists find it hard to assign a section of language to the units or categories they have created. This is known as the token-to-type problem. If you define your types too strictly, it is going to be very difficult to decide later if a particular piece of language is a token of a type or not. If you define your types too loosely, important differences may be lost or concealed. Adjustments can be made later, but the definition of types will stand as a benchmark for the reality of the model. If the terms are too abstract, it will detract from the theory's credibility.

Probably, the most difficult task is to show how the different levels of language interact. To date, the main ideas seem to revolve around an assortment of models. One of the earliest was Saussure's idea of paradigmatic and syntagmatic parameters. Firth envisaged them as coordinates moving through a linguistic space of choices, gradually honing in on an appropriate utterance. Some models are hierarchic with higher levels controlling lower ones. The various levels – phonemes, morphemes, words, phrases, sentences and utterances – are ordered top down with each level subject to dual controls, its own and those above it. An example is Lamb's stratificational grammar. The advent of computers introduced the notion of networks. The interconnections of networks can range three-dimensionally, but still combine the notion of levels. With generative grammar, the image changes to a fountain or an inverted pyramid. Near the base, there are a finite number of rules governing the creation of sentences that fan out and up to the surface as utterances. Another model is of a spherical web. At its centre are a set of core beliefs that are protected from change. These are the inviolable laws of thought that form the basis of logic. At the periphery are their less essential manifestations that absorb the changes that the passage of time forces. Quine's web of belief is representative of this kind of model. Last are flow models. These envisage pathways along which there are points at which separate processes of conversion take place that eventually lead to encoding or decoding speech.

Let's now look at an internalist theory. We shall use generative grammar as an example because it will allow us to dig a little deeper into some of the points raised in the last chapter and, also, because Chomsky is the one claiming that externalist theories are not scientific.

An Internalist Theory

For this description, we shall draw from *Language and Unconscious Knowledge* which was published in *Rules and Representations* in 1980. It forms one of a group of lectures given at Columbia University that are generally acknowledged as among Chomsky's best. The text is tight and extremely well organized. Since no paraphrasing would do it justice, quotations will form the narrative interspersed with comments.

Chomsky begins by complaining that 'language' is too vague a concept for fruitful investigation. He cites the blurred borderline between languages and dialects as one reason. Although it is not made clear, this should be read as: too vague for the kind of investigation he has in mind. After all, **dialectologists** (those who study dialects) have not been distracted from their investigations by this fact.

Chomsky goes on to say that he is going to put forward an abstract idea (the hypothesis) as a starting point. He states that this is not unusual in the natural sciences and cites Galileo as a famous precursor of this method. It was Galileo who first put forward the, then outrageous, idea that it was not the Sun that revolved the Earth, but the planets that revolved the Sun. Chomsky dubs this method the 'Galilean style'. He justifies this deductive approach of working from a general idea to discovering individual facts on the grounds that, one, the mind is so complex, two, progress has stalled in linguistics and radical idealizations are needed, and, three, we have to abstract away from variations. He states, 'Any serious study, abstracts away from variation [that is] tentatively regarded as insignificant' (219). We should note here that 'serious' indicates attitude. Many sociolinguists would argue that variation tells us something very profound about language. But Chomsky backs this statement up by portraying the alternative as uninteresting, 'a form of natural history, tabulation and arrangement of facts, hardly a very serious pursuit however engaging the data' (219).

The result of abstracting away leads to a competence model of language. He concedes that this is controversial, but asks us to imagine 'an ideal homogeneous speech community' (219) in which there is no variation in style or dialect. The next assumption is that knowledge of language is 'uniformly represented in the mind of each of its members, as one element in a system of cognitive structures' (220). From this follows a key statement: this representation in the mind is the grammar of the language. The linguist's theory of grammar will model that mental grammar. The theory will be correct only insofar as it corresponds to the internally represented grammar (220). Jumping ahead a little, he admits 'the limitations of feasible experiment' for this correlation between the model and the mental reality (227), but adds that this is not unusual in the natural sciences. We should note that the alliance he claims between linguistics and the natural sciences is not as uncontroversial as he makes out.

He then goes on to describe his conception of grammar. The grammar will determine the properties of each of the sentences of a language, the phonetic form, meaning and perhaps more. He states, 'The language is the set of sentences that are described by the grammar' (220). We should note that sentences are not like the utterances of speech, but are conceived of as grammatically well-formed. This is what makes his conception of language so grammatical. He goes on to say that the language generated by the grammar is infinite, but the rules of the grammar are finite. To explain how a finite number of rules can generate an infinite variety of sentences, he states, 'the rules of grammar must iterate in some manner' (221–222). We make use of this recursive property to understand new sentences in novel circumstances 'generally bringing much more than our knowledge of language to the performance of these creative acts' (222). This leads up to his contention that because language is not controlled by stimuli the 'creative aspect of language use' must be a species property of humans. He draws a distinction between the generation of sentences by the grammar and the production and interpretation of those sentences by language users. The grammar simply characterizes the intrinsic physical and semantic properties of those sentences. Jumping ahead again, this distinction will be described as the difference between grammatical and pragmatic competence (224). The latter, as subject matter, is then described as offering, 'no promising approach to the normal creative use of language' or 'to any other rule-governed human acts that are freely undertaken' (222). It may, however, be more effective in describing what successful communication is or what 'a logic of conversation' might be (225). He is quieter on the question of the functions of language, only remarking that they might be interesting where they determine rules (230). But he lumps together attempts to show the 'essential purpose of language is to achieve instrumental ends, to satisfy needs' as lacking any substantive proposals (230). On the other hand, 'the study of grammar raises problems that we have some hope of solving' while 'the creative use of language' will always be 'a mystery that eludes our intellectual grasp' (222). He considers possible objections, notions of normal behaviour, for example, but finds no grounds to change his opinion. He returns to his main contention, the hypothesis: 'At an appropriate level of abstraction, we hope to find deep explanatory principles underlying the generation of sentences by grammars' (224–225). The discovery of these principles will justify the idealizations. The latter, then, is the litmus test of the veracity of his theory. Later he states, 'These rules and principles are in large measure unconscious and beyond the reach of potential consciousness' (231). One wonders what possible corroboration there could be for such principles. Undeterred, he goes on to argue that the mind is the place of study for language. This leads him to disparage previous empirical approaches such as behavioural psychology. He states his conviction clearly: 'human language is a system with recursive structure-dependent rules, operating on sequences organized in a hierarchy of phrases to generate a countable infinity of sentences' (239–240).

The article continues, but our account will stop here. Now let's turn our attention to an externalist theory of language.

An Externalist Theory

We shall use systemic grammar as an example of an externalist theory. It may not be typical, but its emphasis on the uses to which language is put makes it externalist. The fundamental concept of this grammar is that language is a system of networks that formalizes the notion of choice and that the choices made serve the construction and construal of meaning. Two of Halliday's articles will be used. They are *Syntax and the Consumer* written in 1964 and *Systemic Grammar and the Concept of a Science of Language* written in 1992. The page references below are drawn from Halliday (2003) in which both papers were reprinted. As with

Chomsky's paper, it will be impossible to do justice to the detail, but our focus will be on those parts that relate to the scientific features listed earlier. We shall begin with the first paper.

Halliday begins by arguing for the equality of different models of language according to their aims. He then lists criteria that substantiate this egalitarian view: (i) different descriptions follow from different models, (ii) different models conceal similarities and differences among themselves, (iii) models impose different kinds of descriptions and (iv) descriptions may differ because linguists differ in their interpretation of the facts (39). He offers two examples of how T-G grammar and his own system, then called scale-and-category, differ in their explanation of active and passive sentences and how questions are formed.

He then goes on to describe the aim of his work as showing 'the patterns inherent in the linguistic performance of the native speaker' (40). This is 'what we mean by "how the language works" ' (40). This involves a general description of those patterns the linguist thinks 'primary in the language' (40) and it entails describing the special features of varieties (registers), statistical properties and the comparison of texts, spoken and written. This information is useful for literary scholarship, native and foreign language teaching, educational research, sociological and anthropological studies and medical applications. The focus is not on 'what the native speaker knows of his language' but 'what he does with it' (40).

Already we discern significant differences. Halliday is dealing with a performance model of language and wants the description and aims of the model to be useful not just for linguistics but applications outside of linguistics (46). This encapsulates the difference between **applied** and **pure linguistics**. Between the lines, we also sense that he is aware of the strong claims being made for T-G grammar at that time – as if it represented the final analysis. He writes, 'we should not take it for granted that a description in terms of a formalized model,' which lacks certain properties that other models have 'will necessarily be the best description for all' of the various purposes of language (38).

Gradually, he moves into a discussion of the criteria adopted for token-to-type assignment. This is difficult, but important. It is the nuts-and-bolts. If you get this wrong, everything goes pear-shaped. He describes 'a scale of delicacy' his team has devised to analyse texts. It sounds like a set of guidelines to help them towards consistency in their assignment of tokens to types. The clause has been chosen as one of the types. Halliday remarks that T-G grammar seems to have opted for a safe option by choosing the sentence as the type (41). He points out that this choice has no criteria, but then wonders whether it reflects a desire for a description that native speakers find easy to recognize. He notes that token-to-type assignment is where native speaker's intuitions tend to be most uncertain. Possibly because of this difficulty, he believes a 'both yes and no' category to be useful (42). We can note two things here, one, this category is not going to please formalists who expect everything to be sorted into absolute categories, and, two, just what percentage of the analysis finds itself in this neither-nor basket will be important.

Moving on to the second article, Halliday begins by saying that it is natural for linguists to emulate the practices of the natural sciences because they have been so successful. He thinks this is good because it helps towards an objective description. But he argues that language is different: it is a semiotic system of the type that construes meaning and a science of meaning is going to be very different to a science of nature or society. In this, we see that Halliday does not see as strong a connection between linguistics and natural science as Chomsky does. He views language meanings as **indeterminate** (fuzzy, open to interpretation). This is another reason for the 'both yes and no' category.

He then goes on to say that he is not trying to prove that linguistics is a science as the title of the paper might suggest, but only wishes to describe what principles and practices he and his colleagues follow. He lists 13 points. We shall not consider all of them, but only enough to satisfy our intention.

The first and third points concern the choice of names used for the categories of his grammar. Halliday explains how they try to give names that show the general purpose of the part of language they are describing and that they are defined in relation to one another.

The second point explains that systemic grammar has two categories, theoretical and descriptive. As examples of the first, he lists metafunction, system, level, class and realization. As examples of the second, he lists clause, preposition, Subject, material process and Theme. Immediately, we sense that if we are to understand this theory, we must first master the meanings of these technical terms. But we then realize that they will only be understood in the context of the theory. A small thing to ask, one might think. But there is a problem. The reason we cannot understand them as they stand is because, as stated earlier, they have been defined in relation to one another. This is typical of dependence theories – those that describe a network where each factor depends on another. But the drawback is if every element depends upon others, there is no single factor that can be touted as the lynchpin. This can affect the popularization of a theory because singular images are what the media love. They can be reproduced easily, network complexities cannot.

Point four is very interesting because it contrasts functional types of grammar to formal kinds. It shows how differences in choice of level and unit result in significantly different descriptions. Systemic grammar identifies its descriptive terms from three perspectives – (1) above, (2) around, and (3) below (203). If my interpretation is correct, the third level corresponds to the smallest descriptive units, for example, in phrase structure grammar, the constituents – articles, adjectives, nouns, etc. The top level refers to the functions (requests, commands, etc.) attributed to the sentence structures selected by systemic grammarians for the third level.

The second level is about what goes with what inside the grammar itself. It seems that formal grammars give priority to the third level, whereas functional grammars prioritize the first level with the third level typically derived from it. Halliday argues that any level can be selected and given prominence but that they all involve compromise, especially if one attempts to give equal weight to all three.

Points six, seven and eight all concern the usefulness of systemic grammar in bilingual comparisons, and the description of other languages in terms of its theoretical architecture. The account is very thorough and it is obvious Halliday has had hands-on experience in applying his system to other languages.

Point nine relates how real language texts and instances of spoken and written language are used as data for description and that large quantities of natural text are processed on computers. These computer corpuses enable them to base the grammar on what people actually say and to undertake large-scale quantitative studies of grammatical patterns and explain the grammar in terms of probabilities.

How Do these Theories Relate to Scientific Criteria?

Despite both theories setting out to explain the same phenomenon, it is amazing how different they are. Their differences reflect, one, what they count as data, two, what problems have motivated their analysis and, three, how they think they can answer those problems. Despite the difficulties, let's try to relate them to the features we listed earlier as typical of science. We shall merge some of those features and consider them in the following order – hypothesis, method, selection of data, formulization, reasoning and discovery of principles/rules.

Hypothesis. Chomsky's basic hypothesis is that a FL exists and that a true theory of grammar models it. It is a bold claim, but it is conceivable that some part of language might be genetically encoded in the brain's neural circuitry. It is going to be very difficult to investigate, however. But that point will be taken up under method. Halliday's hypothesis was inherited from his mentor, J. R. Firth. Based on the observation of language, a hypothesis was formed: language is the uses to which it is put. The hypothesis has an air of common sense about it. The overall 'meaning' of language is its uses. Specifically, the aim was to explain language by linking its structural patterns to their social functions.

Method. When it comes to testing his hypothesis, Chomsky chooses particular instances that he believes will reveal evidence for structure-dependency rules. There are many questions surrounding the effectiveness of this method. Here are some. Are the particular instances of language chosen so far sufficient to demonstrate the claims made? How much can data output really tell us about the inside of the 'black box'? There is no evidence that internal organization must match output. Thirdly, how safe are the rules adduced from native speaker's intuitive judgements? Despite these objections, as we shall see, some very interesting results have been uncovered.

Halliday tests the hypothesis by creating networks of semantic choices to show that language operates as claimed. In the assignment of token to type, his method also relies on intuition, this time it is mainly the intuition of professional linguists. From a hard-nosed scientific point of view, it is not very satisfactory because it introduces subjective interpretation of the data. But what else is on offer? Even computers only follow instructions.

Selection of data. In the selection of data, we see the clearest difference between the two theories: Chomsky eliminates variables, Halliday deals with a pimples-and-all performance model. Although Chomsky believes he has fully justified his decision to deal with a highly idealized competence model, this has attracted a lot of criticism from those working with a performance model. If we ask just how much linguistic data has been omitted from his model, the answer must be everything that is not grammatical. And that's a lot. It excludes all spoken language that does not form grammatically correct sentences, most poetry, variants and anything that is non-standard. Halliday's choice to deal with language as it is used has created difficulties, but he believes he has put in place working guidelines to minimize the negative effects of wide variation in the data. For example, all deviant or non-standard uses of language are labelled.

Formulization. Chomsky's grammar should be easier to formulate than Halliday's because he has eliminated variation. But what fraction of all the rules of language do the rules that have been formulated represent? This question is not meant to detract from the achievement of generativists, but the answer must be only a fraction since the data has been limited to those parts of language that are most clearly rule-governed. Halliday views language as inherently indeterminate. This means he believes that probably only a part of language could ever lend itself to being formulated. Even so, findings have been formulated in terms of statistics, especially regarding frequency and quantification. He mentions the Penman text generation project and gives some impressive examples of quantification (2003: 407–411).

Reasoning. Both theorists shape their theories according to their doctrinaire preferences. Chomsky's draws on the rationalist tradition and Halliday's on the empiricist. Because Chomsky's claims went in the face of earlier empirical behaviourist thinking on language, he had to provide a philosophical case for his research program. Halliday accepted the empirical contention of language's close links to behaviour. His credentials are made plain in statements like, 'once we recognize that the grammar of every natural language is itself a theory of experience' (2003: 392). In short, he argues that aspects of grammar such as mood, tense, etc. are shaped by the human experience. He gives a well-argued account and probability figures for how many times children have heard certain patterns of language in an attempt to narrow the gap that Chomsky claims exists between stimuli and the child's knowledge of language.

Principles and rules. Researchers following directions set by Chomsky have come up with a number of new and genuine rules of grammar. Two that are frequently cited are *The Precede-and-Command Condition* and *The Complex Noun Phrase Constraint* because they are relatively easy to explain. The first is a rule governing the use of pronouns, the second concerns the circumstances in which it is possible to form questions. Other rules about, for example, adverbs and functional heads, clausal structures and so on, are far more technical. They cannot be neatly reduced to simple formulae probably because there are too many exceptions or special cases. But some formalists argue there is a growing body of evidence for parameters that could form the principles of UG. It is probably fair to say that more time is needed to assess those claims.

Halliday's view of language as an inherently indeterminate social semiotic system means that he is not searching for the same kind of rules as generativists. He searches for quantitative evidence of statistical effects. For example, how the most common 50 verbs in English account for 90 per cent of all verb occurrences, how active verbs occur about 10 times more frequently than passive ones (2003: 27). He is mainly interested in frequency occurrence and functional variation which have practical applications for language learning.

Conclusion

What then are we to make of Chomsky's claim that externalist theories are not as scientific as his? While there may be some that trade in generalizations, Halliday's is not one of them. It is as scientific as Chomsky's, albeit from an empirical rather than a rationalist standpoint. We do not have to resolve the pros and cons of empiricism and rationalism here, but it seems that Chomsky's rock-solid certainty about how linguistics should be for any 'serious' linguist has led him to be too absolute in his judgements. Internalist and externalist theories could form two sides of the same coin. Despite this, there are few voices in linguistics today arguing for a theory that could unify both views.

Other questions which remain controversial are, first, is the link between linguistics and natural science as uncontroversial as Chomsky maintains? He argues that it is up to those who think it is controversial to explain why. But tradition has already stated their views. It goes something like this: physicists have something in front of their eyes, an entity under a microscope, for example. The object of enquiry has matter which is why it is called a physical science. When linguistics is treated as a mental science, it is trying to describe a place inside our heads that cannot be seen. Some might object that CAT (computerized axial tomography), MRI (magnetic resonance imagery) and PET (positron emission tomography) scans of language activity in the brain are on a par with the photographed traces that scientists use to explain the behaviour of subatomic particles. But there is a difference: there is nothing in our nerve tissue that resembles language. Add to this the fact that the study of language is carried out both in and by means of language and you have a problem. When the object of study is the same as the tool of investigation and explanation it affects the degree of objectivity. This is the Achilles' heel of linguistic theory. While the same problem may exist in other sciences, it is not as acute. Put simply, it is a situation that compromises science.

The second question is, how well have the relative contributions of grammar, lexicon and phonology to semantics been explained? It is widely recognized that generative grammars give priority to syntax and that syntax is not all there is to semantics. But there we must stop. The scope of semantics is so broad that we must postpone our discussion of it until the next chapter.

Chapter 6: *In this chapter, we considered the main features of scientific enquiry. The purpose of this was to assess Chomsky's claims that externalist explanations of language were less scientific than his own. Then we outlined the main tenets of two theories – one internalist, the other externalist. The former was Chomsky's generative grammar, the latter Halliday's systemic grammar. We then compared them in terms of scientific features. We reached the conclusion that both are scientific, albeit from different standpoints.*

Study Question

Just for a bit of fun, fill in the chart shown in Figure 20. 3 points stands for 'very good', 2 for 'good', and 1 for 'not so good'. Total up the score in each column and find out which of the two theories you think is more scientific according to this brief presentation of the facts.

	Generative grammar	Systemic grammar
hypothesis		
methods of testing		
selection of data		
formulization		
reasoning		
discovery of principles/rules		
Total		

Figure 20 Which is more scientific?

Chapter 7: *In the next chapter, we shall consider semantics and ask what has made the subject so complicated.*

What Makes Semantics Difficult?

Introduction

Of the three main branches of linguistics, **semantics** (the study of meaning) has been most neglected. It has been pushed to one side for a number of reasons, but mainly because it is thought to be inherently subjective in the way it introduces a host of intractable variables such as feelings, intentions and beliefs. These variables can affect the literal meaning of what a person says. Meanings can also be affected by non-linguistic factors such as situation and context of utterance. As we said in the last chapter, subjectivity is the bane of science because it prevents observers from finding a neutral viewpoint from which everything appears the same for everyone. Because of this subjective dimension, semantics defies a totally scientific description.

This chapter will act as a general introduction to various views as to what meaning might be. Its aim is threefold: one, to show how and why the subject has become so muddled; two, to provide a ground plan to help students know where they are in this maze; and three, to lay the groundwork for following chapters so that we may probe more deeply into some of the issues.

The first and most obvious complicating factor is that meaning is the concern not of one, but many disciplines. So the first thing we shall do is name the main players.

Too Many Cooks Spoil the Broth

Perhaps it would be fairer to say that the importance of meaning has attracted the attention of many great thinkers. From fields as diverse as mathematics and poetry, they have flocked like pilgrims to find the source of its spring. But the effect of so much attention has, unwittingly, culminated into a spoiling one. It has created a labyrinth of Byzantine complexity. The three main contributors to this bewildering maze are philosophy, semiotics and linguistics. Because the focus and motivation for their interest varies so widely, their differences cannot be summarized easily. Let's consider the first two briefly and then linguistics in more detail.

Philosophy enters the picture because the answers to so many of its questions depend upon the meaning of the words they are expressed in. There are three branches of philosophy interested in meaning: philosophy of language, philosophy of mind and **epistemology** (theory of knowledge). Philosophy of language asks how meaning can be. Philosophy of mind answers by claiming that the operations of language are mental, that is governed by thought. Epistemology asks what kind of knowledge our minds allow. It is particularly interested in the kind of knowledge expressed in **propositions**. Propositions take the form of subject plus predicate. For example, in the proposition 'Sugar is sweet', 'Sugar' is the subject and 'is sweet' the predicate. Propositions like these express a relationship between the predicate and the subject that seems to mirror a fundamental divide we see in nature. In particular, the way we attribute qualities to entities. If that correspondence is correct, then the proposition is true, if not, then false. In this way, truth, with a capital T, comes centre stage.

These three branches of philosophy introduce three kinds of theories that are virtually inseparable. Philosophy of language constructs theories of meaning which are also sometimes called theories of understanding. Philosophy of mind constructs theories of what we are cognizant of which cannot help but form the background to theories of meaning and understanding. Epistemology creates theories of truth and these, too, spill into theories of knowledge and meaning. Like the witches in Macbeth, they form a beguiling trio.

Semiotics has several different takes on meaning. The main are cultural. One version is **hermeneutics** which is concerned with texts and the discovery of new interpretations. More traditional approaches concern the nature of the sign. These will be considered in the next chapter. Newer approaches stem from **cybernetics** (a new science of communication particularly interested in automated control systems such as those of living organisms) and **systems theory** (a transdisciplinary study of organization).

Before we turn to linguistics, two points should be noted. The first is that these three subjects are not like islands: they form connections and influence one another. The ideas of philosophers, in particular, filter into other subjects, subtly affecting them over time. Often they provide the grounds for positions on fundamental questions. The second point which follows from the first is that whenever one picks up a book on meaning it is advisable to read the author's profile. Is s/he a philosopher, psychologist, linguist, neurophysiologist? Their background will determine the focus of their enquiry, the kind of questions they are interested in answering, and how they frame them.

Let's now turn our attention to linguistics to continue our exploration of how semantics has become difficult terrain.

Divisions and Subdivisions

Numerous divisions and subdivisions have been created for the study of meaning. The major one concerns the meaning of the word 'mean'. In English, 'mean' can mean 'intend' or 'be equivalent to'. The first meaning can be applied to speakers and writers, people who use language. The second is used of words and sentences. For example, when someone asks, 'What does *schadenfreude* mean?'

This first division should never be lost sight of. It boils down to a simple question: Are we talking about what speakers mean or what words and sentences mean? The former concerns what a speaker intends to convey when they use language. The latter concerns what a sentence means, or what counts as its equivalent in a language. The very real gap that exists between them can easily be demonstrated. The sentence, 'My feet are killing me' can be used by the same or different speakers on different occasions to mean (intend) different things. A soldier in the rage of battle could mean it literally. A shopper could mean it metaphorically.

Metaphorical meanings are more closely associated with associative meanings that have attached themselves to the core, literal, or denotative, meanings of words. They exist at the periphery, the borders of a word's semantic territory. When the boss tells the workforce to 'Pull your socks up', you know s/he wants everyone to work harder not to literally heave their socks higher. Literal meanings are more closely related to aspects of meaning determined by the language system.

A direct consequence of this first division accounts for another important division – the kind of data that linguists are dealing with. Those interested in the study of literal meaning only concern themselves with **sentence** meaning. This has the effect of idealization, of abstracting language from its living context. On the other hand, those interested in the will of speakers and circumstances of use, context, situation, etc. will study **utterances**. Utterances are not like sentences. Whereas sentences are grammatically complete and are considered to embody one complete thought, utterances can be phrases ('Another cuppa?' 'Me, too.' 'Heads or tails?'), interjections ('Eh?'), and so on. They are grammatically incomplete, but still communicate in situation. Semantics has chosen the path of literal meaning, while pragmatics prefers to study meaning in situation.

Never forgetting this first most important division, let's now look at finer divisions within semantics (as opposed to pragmatics).

Specializations

Although **semanticity** (meaningfulness) depends upon the interaction of three systems – the lexicon, the grammar and phonology – there is, naturally, a tendency for linguists to specialize in only one of these. This is because there is enough information in just one aspect to occupy a lifetime of study. Not surprisingly, and often unintentionally, specializing can result in a one-sided view. For example, if only written data is under scrutiny, the prosodic features of a sentence can easily be forgotten. Intonation can change the meaning of sentences. For example, someone could say, 'Very interesting' in an ironic tone and change the literal meaning to its exact opposite. Or they could make a statement into a question by saying it with a rising tone – 'You are going?' In tonal languages, different tones are used to change the meaning of words that share the same sound. In this way, other aspects that contribute to meaning can be obscured.

The aspect of meaning that is most important to semantics is the fact that language has structure. This is sometimes referred to as its **compositionality**. Put simply, if sentences are not composed properly they lose their meaning. For example, if someone said, 'Mat on the cat the sat', it would be gibberish. In contrast, sentences like Chomsky's oft-quoted 'Colorless green ideas sleeping furiously' appear to make sense, but, in fact, do not. These examples illustrate two axes of meaning – the grammatical and the lexical. In the first, the word order is wrong and it is ungrammatical. In the second, the word order is correct but the words make no sense. Two different lines of semantic research have emerged from these aspects of compositionality – lexical and formal.

Lexical semantics concerns substitutional possibilities, while **formal semantics** concerns combinatorial possibilities. Their differences have led them to present particular views of meaning. Lexical semantics presents meanings as choices among words and phrases. This paradigmatic approach represents networks of organization rather than clear hierarchical systems. Semanticists of a formal persuasion prefer the syntagmatic, or combinatorial, approach. Typically, they reduce the paradigmatic dimension to the syntagmatic by assigning words to grammatical classes on the grounds that they regularly occur in the same place. By doing so, formal semanticists can make it seem that the computational operations of syntax are all there is to meaning. This is why many question how well formal models have integrated semantics. They argue that if lexical variations are ignored, then a false picture emerges.

When a subject becomes as fragmented as this, it is useful to look at its history to find out how so many divisions arose. So let's now turn our attention to an historical account of these divisions.

Historical Background

In his introduction to Derrida's *Speech and Phenomena*, Newton Garver writes that the study of language used to be divided by the theologians of the medieval period into three divisions – grammar, logic and rhetoric. The three divisions correspond to three skills we expect of a language user. We expect a person to be able to form sentences correctly – grammatical competence. We expect a person to recognize when an expression is absurd or contradictory or illogical – logical competence. And we expect a person to know when and how to use a linguistic expression whose grammar and logic they have understood – rhetorical competence. Although it is not immediately apparent, there is a conflict of interest in this tripartite division between logic and rhetoric.

Historically, the scope of rhetorical studies has come to be restricted to public speeches, literature, and the classification of styles, etc. However, the wider, less traditional, understanding of its remit is the study of the appropriateness or inappropriateness of various expressions in various sorts of circumstances, including the proper use of contradictory expressions. It is here that rhetoric comes into conflict with logic. The difference between the two is, briefly, that the study of sentences in logic proceeds formally; that is, without taking account of time, place or circumstance of use. It idealizes away from the actual situation of use. Rhetoric, on the other hand, takes these factors into account in its consideration of logic.

While French intellectuals have tended to support rhetoric, most of Anglo-American philosophy has been based on logic. Modern philosophy of language has also been more concerned with a theory of meaning based on logic. This is due to the enormous influence of five great thinkers – Frege, Husserl, Russell, Whitehead and Wittgenstein. Rhetoric's alternative conception of language – for example, Rousseau's claims that the origin of language lay in the rhythms and intonations of our emotions rather than in the logical – have remained in the shadows. All of the philosophers mentioned, excepting the later work of Husserl, Whitehead and Wittgenstein, associated problems of language with problems of mathematics and as basically logical in character.

The dominance of the logical account of language has had the following consequences. First, the actual came to be explained in terms of the ideal. The ideal (timeless, context-free) semantic relation of signs to one another could be separated from the (time-dependent, contextually variant) semantic relations of signs to the world. This created a division in semantics in which the meaning of linguistic expressions became one sort of question and how and when they were applied a separate, independent question. From this, arose divisions such as formal/functional and semantic/pragmatic.

The formal has tended to reinforce the association of language meaning to logic. For example, Chomsky's search for the logical formulations of language exemplifies this approach. His Cartesian linguistics points to the static purity of logic and its forms as prior to experience. Functional approaches find their expression in sociolinguistics, pragmatics and discourse studies. In Hasan's words, they are concerned with how 'language is used for the living of life' (qtd. in Coupland et al. 2001: 19).

Against this background of underlying causes for present-day divisions, let's look at other developments that have complicated the study of meaning. The first concerns disagreement over how the atom of meaning – the linguistic sign – should be split.

Splitting the Atom of Meaning

While most agree that the linguistic sign, word or symbol is the atom of meaning, not all agree on how many parts it contains. In the literature, its parts are termed **dimensions**, **relata** or **correlates**. Among semantic theories, some explain the sign in terms of only one dimension. These are termed **monist** accounts. However, most propose two, three or even more dimensions: these are termed, respectively, **dualist, triadic** or **pluralist**. The most commonly discussed dimensions are those of **sense** and **reference**. In terms of the dimension of sense, meaning is usually defined as a concept. As a reference, it is an act of thinking of, or referring to, a referent, object, entity or state of affairs. As a **relation**, it is a function that operates either between reference and sense, reference and its user, or reference and other signs.

These terms are used in linguistics, semiotics and philosophy. But students should be wary: these are not the only terms used for the sign's dimensions and, even where they are, definitions can vary widely among writers. Semiotician Winfried Nöth hits the nail on the head when he describes the 'jungle of terms' for the dimensions of the sign as a 'Babylonian confusion' (1995: 92/93).

Approaches to meaning via the reference/sense relation can be broadly divided into those that claim it is direct and those that claim it is indirect. These approaches reflect different philosophical schools of thought on how direct our perception of reality is.

Direct views emphasize reference over sense, while indirect views reverse the emphasis. Let's consider the direct view first.

The Direct View

This view maintains there is a direct link between words and their senses and referents. Its origin can be traced to Plato (427–347 BC) who argued that the world we live in is populated by imperfect manifestations of a 'pure' world of ideal forms. Here, 'pure' means unrelated to earthly experience. You will remember that rationalists argue that we cannot rely on the evidence of our senses because they are of the illusory world of appearances. They want to go directly through reasoning to the principles that govern the reality behind the natural world of appearances. Views, like Plato's, are described as unmediated, **iconic** (based on similarity or resemblance) and non-arbitrary because of the direct link they maintain the sign has to its ideal form.

One of the reasons Plato argued for such a timeless realm was because he believed in reincarnation. He thought previous existences had already acquainted us with the eternal ideas of mathematics, virtue and so on. However, even he was not entirely happy with his theory. What about trivial entities like 'tables', 'bags' and 'dirt'? Did they, too, exist in that ideal realm? Despite not many people believing in reincarnation these days, there are modern versions of Platonism. Semantic theorists Jerrold Katz (b. 1932) and Jerry Fodor (b. 1935) argue that actual linguistic forms derive from a world of pure linguistic forms which are similar to the numbers and sets of mathematics, and that they are mind-independent and accessed by a non-sensory intuition (Brown et al. 2002: 393). Even Chomsky, writing in 1991 on the acquisition of concepts, agreed with this view while admitting it seemed preposterous. He claimed that concepts such as 'chase', 'persuade', 'murder' are innate, that is prior to experience (Wierzbicka 1996: 18).

According to semanticist William Frawley, adherents of an iconic theory of grammar also argue that linguistic categories – nouns, verbs, etc. – are a kind of signifier that reflect ideal semantic forms; for example, that nouns universally encode entities, verbs encode temporally dynamic relations, etc. It is difficult to substantiate such claims. Chinese, for example, does not use verbs to encode tense.

The Indirect View

The indirect view argues that the connection between word and object is mediated, noniconic or opaque. This position can be traced back to Aristotle (384–322 BC) who claimed that the relation between words and their objects is conventional and that social rules determine how meanings are paired with words. It is also arbitrary because it is not motivated by resemblance to the thing it names, but wholly symbolic insofar as it stands for that thing. It is to this tradition that Saussure's structuralism belongs.

Figure 21 illustrates one version of this view. The dotted line indicates that there is no direct relation between the word and its referent – it is mediated through the sense of the word in the system of language. Some other terms typically used for the sign's dimensions are given. In triadic models such as these, the three

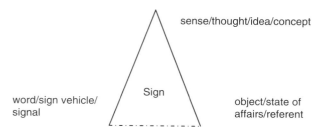

Figure 21 The semiotic triangle

dimensions combine to form a sign, to which, by definition, meaning adheres. The strong point of triadic models is that they acknowledge the objects of reality as a part of the picture. Their drawback is that they exclude the role of the interpreter and context.

The difference between this account of the linguistic sign and Saussure's should be carefully noted: Saussure's sign is a psychological entity of two inseparable dimensions – the sound-image (an imprint of sound) linked to its concept. Although essentially mental, it has a spoken mode. Against this immanent view of meaning, traditional referential semantics argued that it was impossible to study phenomena of a **deictic** kind (those that have a personal, temporal or spatial aspect and depend on context of utterance) without having recourse to the dimension of reference. Those who believed there was no direct link between word and object responded by asking their critics to show them what words such as *Pegasus, soul* and *the* referred to.

The direct view is named the **realist** position in philosophy and the indirect view **representative realism**. How could a school of thought that argued for an ideal realm or some similar approximation come to be called 'realist'? Contemporary philosopher Roger Scruton puts it like this, 'you are a "realist" about x if you think x exists independently of our thoughts about it' (2004: 31).

Presumably, the importance of this debate about the sign's relationship to reality lies in the following distinction: if meaning was in a direct relation, our judgements would be on surer grounds than if it were working on indirect sensations. But this question can be ignored, because, whichever it is, direct or indirect, it changes nothing. It is all we have to go on. A car hurtling towards you should convince you of this. All it probably indicates is that we are capable of a shift of attention: we can switch from perceiving something directly to a less forceful, and therefore seemingly indirect, contemplation of its image or memory after the event.

The next difficulty we shall consider is the sheer number of approaches to the question of meaning.

Which Door Should I Go Through?

There are many different starting points that reflect different aims and approaches to the question of meaning. Eight of the main approaches have been selected and listed in the left column of Figure 22. In the middle column, the type of semantic theory associated with the approach is shown and, in the right column, the names of various associated semantic theories. The list is by no

Approaches to Meaning	Type of Semantics	Associated theories
As reference (1)	referential formal logical lexical functional	truth-conditional, verificationist, generative, model-theoretical, natural semantic metalanguage, systemic grammar
As sense (2)	conceptualist	structuralist, or associationist
As context (3)	pragmatic	context-and-use, speech act theory
As concept (4)	cognitive	experientialist synthesis, symbolic thesis
As intentionality	psychological	phenomenological
As culture	anthropological poststructuralist postmodernist sociological	Sapir-Whorf Hypothesis, generalized theories of meaning, French discourse analysis, deconstructionism. praxis theory, structural functional
As behaviour	psychological	stimulus-response
As organism	(bio) semiotic	systems theory, autopoiesis theory, Whitehead's philosophy of the organism

Figure 22 Main approaches to the study of meaning

means exhaustive. Looking down the list, the reader should not assume that there is a one-to-one relation between the type of semantic theory and the associated theory because they share the same line.

When there are as many approaches as this a choice must be made. In what follows, four approaches that bear most usefully on language have been chosen. They are meaning as reference, as sense, as context and as concept. How 'concept' differs from 'sense' will become clearer later.

Meaning as Reference

The modern history of meaning as reference begins with the German philosopher Gottlob Frege (1848–1925). Frege was first and foremost a mathematician who wanted to prove that mathematics was not a priori knowledge. Unlike realists of a Platonic persuasion, he believed in the objective reality of mathematical objects. He wanted to bring it down to earth by plucking it out of Plato's transcendental realm. To do this, he set about showing how it could be reduced to logic. The upshot of his work was **predicate logic** – an artificial language which is used to make clear the logical connections of sentences.

His ideas gradually began to influence linguistics. That meaning can be computed by combining the meaning of the parts of a sentence underlies the notion of **compositionality** (the notion of parts contributing to the whole), sometimes referred to as **Frege's principle** or the **context principle**. This principle made word-meaning secondary to sentence-meaning. The belief that there is congruence between grammatical structure and logical form also led to the analysis of meaning in terms of whether it was true or false. The favourite kind of sentence for this sort of analysis was the proposition. This is because it introduces a relationship between the subject and predicate that can either be true or false.

A proposition was true if it corresponded to the state of affairs it referred to and false if it did not. Most propositions are declarative, that is they declare something about something or some collection of things. This is why meaning came to be construed as reference. These views developed into **truth-conditional semantic theory**.

Although Frege's ideas were hugely influential, it was not long before others began to point out that not all propositions refer in a clear way. This is especially true of those that contain an indefinite noun phrase. For example, 'Geoff wants to marry a Vietnamese'. Is Geoff thinking of a particular person or not? It is ambiguous. There are also many sentences that do not form propositions and many sentences whose truth cannot be verified. For example, sentences about the future. As the links of propositions to clear cases of reference became weaker, so, too, did the view that reference was all there was to meaning. In such cases, the role of context becomes more important.

It was the translation of Frege's work that introduced the terms 'sense' (*Sinn*) and 'reference' (*Bedeutung*) to describe the dimensions of meaning. Frege's explanation of these terms underwent changes, but the main version has it that he allotted sense a secondary role to reference. Because of this, his theory is described as referential and, as such, stands firmly within the modern realist tradition. However, it is one thing to choose to give sense a secondary role in order to avoid the pitfalls of the mental aspect of meaning, but quite another thing to ask whether this is truly the case.

Frege's greatest contribution to our understanding of language was to highlight through the development of a formalized metalanguage the logical relations inherent in language and thought. However, his logical approach has what another philosopher, Ludwig Wittgenstein, would later describe as a commitment to a 'private language'. Namely, once linguistic meaning is placed in the domain of logic, it becomes separated. This is because logic, unlike language, cannot vary according to circumstances. It deals with literal meaning on an all-or-nothing basis.

Meaning as Sense

Mentalist theories of meaning are sometimes called **ideational** or **conceptualist** theories. According to these theories, meaning is a concept in the sense of a mental event. Since concepts are associated with signs, such mentalist approaches are termed **associationist theories of meaning**.

The best-known mentalist account of meaning is Saussure's. That branch of linguistics which he founded called **structural semantics** followed the path of locating meaning in the sphere of sense only. Since no structure was admitted beyond the semiotic system of language, the dimension of reference was excluded. This view implies that language structures our perception of the world, and that the senses of words derive their meaning from contrasts within the system of language. This emphasis on language as a relational structure is in stark contrast to referential approaches concerned with truth-correspondences.

Saussure saw language as a system of oppositions, differences and values in which the relations between the signs were more important than the elements of the system. Famously, he stated, 'There are no signs, there are only differences between signs' (qtd. in Nöth 1995: 195). He described two relations between the elements – syntagmatic and paradigmatic relations, and differences and oppositions of values. We shall consider the latter, since the former has been outlined in Chapter 2.

Saussure expressed his concept of meaning by comparing language to a game of chess. He declared that only two things matter in this game: the values of the pieces according to the rules of the game, and their positions on the chessboard. Similarly, he stated 'each linguistic term derives its value from its opposition to all the other terms' (1916: 88). In this metaphor, he is asserting the importance of the relations over the sign elements. Emphasizing this, he wrote that it was only 'differences that make it possible to distinguish [them] from all others, for [only] differences carry signification' (1916: 118). Again, he wrote: 'In language there are only differences *without positive terms*' (1916: 120).

When he does come to characterize the nature of the sign, the basic semiotic element of the system of language, he states that, 'The linguistic sign is arbitrary' and declares this the 'first principle of the nature of the linguistic sign' (67). This was antithetically opposed to Platonic views that claimed the motivated, iconic character of language.

The two main questions that came to the fore in the debate that Saussure's claims sparked were: what is the nature of arbitrariness, and is arbitrariness a matter of sense or reference? Because the meaning of the word 'arbitrary' carries a nuance of free choice, Saussure answered his critics by stating that arbitrariness should be understood as unmotivated. To explain this, he wrote 'There is no reason for preferring *soeur* to *sister*' (1916: 73). In other words, word sounds have no necessary connection to what they signify. This lack of natural connection makes the relation internal to the system, associative (because of differences and oppositions of the values within the system) and mentalist because its emphasis is on the sense dimension of the sign rather than the referent. This last point was very different to Frege's emphasis.

To answer critics who took arbitrariness to imply a freedom of choice regarding the signifier, Saussure stated that arbitrariness accounted for the conventionality of language: 'The arbitrary nature of the sign explains in turn why the social fact alone can create a linguistic system. The community is necessary if values that owe their existence solely to usage and general acceptance are to be set up; by himself the individual is incapable of fixing a single value' (1916: 113). This idea of the fixedness of conventionality underpins Saussure's principle of the **immutability** (unchanging nature) of the sign. This pragmatic, synchronic principle complements his first semantic principle. However, recognizing that language does change over time, he designated another principle, a diachronic one, of linguistic **mutability**.

Because Saussure's theory of the sign strictly excludes any mention of the referent and states that meaning is a matter of sense only, a relation between the two sides of a 'psychological entity', the signifier and the signified, its philosophical position is described as **representative realism**. This kind of realist concedes that there is a world of mind-independent objects that cause us to have experiences, but argue that we do not *directly* perceive them. What we directly perceive are the effects these objects have on us – an internal image, idea or impression. These more or less accurate representations of reality have been called percepts, sense-data, sensations and so on. Saussure called its linguistic manifestation an acoustic image. These sensations in the mind represent (or, when things go wrong, *mis*represent) their external physical causes.

To sum up: for Saussure meaning was a differential value determined by the structure of the language system and not by any extra-linguistic reality. It is a strong argument whose contribution to our understanding of language was to reassert the mental, or psychological, aspect of language as a representational system juxtaposed to social reality. Later, it would be criticized for paying too little attention to syntax.

Meaning as Context – Pragmatic Theories

Pragmatic theories of meaning are those based on the tradition of ordinary-language philosophy that arose as a reaction against the claims of a philosophical movement called **logical positivism** or **logical empiricism** which put forward a semantic theory called **verificationism**. This theory claimed that sentences were meaningful only if they express verifiable or falsifiable propositions. Pragmatic theories can be viewed as rhetoric reclaiming its priority in the study of language.

In contrast to the two approaches outlined above, pragmatic theories argue that meaning is derived from context. Extreme adherents of this view argue that it can only be so derived. Critics think this view is untenable because in any communicative act participants must select meaning from the linguistic expressions on offer and some are non-negotiable. For example, a person may have a choice of vocabulary (big, large, huge, gigantic, humungous, etc.), but the same choice concerning grammatical structure (tense formation, singular–plural distinctions, etc.) does not exist. Views differ on this point since even grammar can vary from one person to another (e.g. 'I don't know nothing'; '[H]'er be daft'). But it seems reasonable to assume that certain choices do not exist.

Because pragmatics is concerned with context and social discourse, the level of analysis changes from sentence to utterance. Other general distinctions between pragmatics and semantics are the manner in which pragmatic theories are more concerned with the effect of the meaning on the hearer, the social basis of language and language as a form of behaviour. These distinctions form its major contribution to our greater understanding of language. Before outlining one pragmatic theory, we shall summarize Wittgenstein's reaction against his earlier views on language since it forms the philosophical foundations of pragmatic theories.

Ordinary-Language Philosophy

Ludwig Wittgenstein (1889–1951) probably did more than anyone to make language central to the concerns of modern philosophy. In his later work, *Philosophical Investigations,* which was written in 1949 and published in English in 1953, he explained meaning in terms of use. This practical view of meaning became known as ordinary-language philosophy.

Attacking the Cartesian theory of mind that emphasized the authority of first-person knowledge, Wittgenstein argued that only a creature that was *part of* the social world could have that kind of personal knowledge. He argued that the rules must be publicly available, or we would never be able to learn them. This goes even for the language of things we normally think of as irreducibly private, 'since a child can learn only from the language and behaviour that he or she observes' (Fearn 2001: 139). His argument effectively undermined the Cartesian position that the mind is a non-physical entity whose states are essentially inner and connected only loosely with outer circumstances. In short, he argued that language was socially instituted – a position very different to Chomsky's.

Wittgenstein developed his argument by stating that 'the thing that determines whether or not one is playing by the rules must be outside oneself, for otherwise it would be too easy to break the rules' (Fearn 2001: 140). He showed that the certainty of truth that Descartes claimed for the first person with his oft-quoted *Cogito ergo sum* ('I think, therefore I am') was derived from the public world of rules of language use. By doing so, he re-established third-person knowledge as equally sure ground for knowledge.

When Wittgenstein stated that 'to imagine a language means to imagine a form of life' he shifted philosophy of language towards an anthropological position. He went on to argue that 'the game itself cannot be true or false: it is merely played or not played' (Fearn 2001: 143). This seems to imply that humans cannot do otherwise than play the 'language game'. He opined that language cannot explain everything because reason must terminate in action – hence the game. Explanation must end in description, something that just 'is the case', a 'given', or it will never end at all.

Wittgenstein's works are extraordinarily profound, and there are many strands of thought that have been, and are still being, extracted from them. Some think that the language games are not as arbitrary as he suggested. Evolutionists think they are there to help us survive in our environment and have adapted to fit our needs. The debate continues. Let's consider one of the first pragmatic theories to develop out of Wittgenstein's thinking.

Speech Act Theory

Speech act theories derive from the ideas of J. L. Austin (1911–1960), an English philosopher who was dissatisfied with the verificationist thesis. Much influenced by Wittgenstein's later works on language as action, he began to analyse utterances and classify them in terms of speech acts, arguing that if you say, for example, 'I promise to pay you £5', you are not saying something is either true or false, but committing yourself to a course of action.

Against this background, he put forward his now famous distinction between **constative** (descriptive) and **performative** utterances. The former is a statement-making utterance. He preferred not to use the more common term 'descriptive' because, in his view, not all true or false statements are descriptive. Performative utterances are those 'in the production of which the speaker, or writer, performs an act of doing rather than saying' (Lyons 1995: 238). Austin went into the question of saying and doing in great detail and developed, if not a full-fledged theory of speech acts, a general theory of pragmatics which explained saying as doing within the framework of social institutions and conventions.

He introduced a number of new terms, such as **locutionary act** and **illocutionary force**. The former produces an utterance with a particular form and a more or less determinate meaning. The product of a locutionary act will have one kind of illocutionary force, for example, a statement, a question, a command, a promise and so on. The relation between the act and the force can be characterized thus $F(p)$, where F is the force and p the proposition or assertion.

How many kinds of speech acts are there? Austin provided a classificatory scheme in *How To Do Things With Words* (1962), but others have been proposed and there is no agreed and definitive version. The most important points to note are speech act theory's links to Wittgenstein's claims that all language must end in action, its more detailed investigation of the role of convention vis-à-vis language, underlying social concepts such as authority and commitment, and the reintroduction of rhetoric to linguistics. It is generally acknowledged that speech act analysis is to a certain extent culture-dependent, and that the illocutionary force of ordinary descriptive statements cannot be accounted for satisfactorily within the framework of truth-conditional semantics.

Meaning as Concept

At the end of the twentieth century, research into meaning took a new turn: it was absorbed into cognitive science. In other words, the direction of research departed from a long philosophical tradition which believed that an account of thought could only be given through an account of language. In linguistics, a similar turn was engineered when Chomsky led research in a psychological direction.

The main exponents of meaning as conceptual structure are George Lakoff, Mark Johnson and Ray Jackendoff. Lakoff and Johnson's theory is called the **experientialist synthesis**. Jackendoff's is termed the Universal Grammar of concepts and is much more closely allied to Chomsky's generative approach. The difference between the two is that the former places less emphasis on innateness than the latter. Both maintain that mind projects the world of reference and attempt to explain truth and reference within a mental model of a projected world. Here we will only consider Lakoff and Johnson's theory.

Lakoff and Johnson argue that language reports input from our five senses and that this forms a universal human cognitive constraint. They believe there must be a convergence of linguistic and non-linguistic information in a central core of conceptual information. This HQ relies upon **categorization** – the construction of mental sets and ideal types – to analyse and report on sensory data. They argue that this is revealed by the fact that linguistic representation is categorical. For example, some languages treat the animate and inanimate differently. In Japanese, you say *iru* if something is living, *aru* if it is a thing. English has 'is' for both. The methodology is to infer from language output to the existence of categories and the structure of concepts. In short, they believe semantic analysis is the same as conceptual analysis, but that the power resides in the structuring of concepts.

The mentally projected world is made up of types – semantic, visual and auditory – and these form the backdrop against which our mental representations are constructed. At the heart of this mental process of categorization are mechanisms that determine similarity (identity) and difference (exclusion or non-identity). This process has been shown to exist with regard to visual categorization. For example, when we look at things we see the smaller thing against a larger background – 'the spoon is in the cup', 'the ladder is by the wall', etc. It is argued that meaning categories are analogously constructed. The appeal of the argument is its simplicity – a single judgement of a fundamental nature, same or different? Some believe the traditional aims of semantics to explain lexical relations such as synonymy, paraphrase, antonymy, contradiction, taxonymy, entailment, inconsistency, redundancy, etc. can all be explained by the mechanisms of mental typing. In short, meaning is a deferential along a continuum of more-or-less like to not-at-all like.

Lakoff and Johnson argue that much of language is structured metaphorically and that this stems from the metaphorical structure of our concepts. By metaphorical, they mean our ability to construe one thing (often an abstract entity) in terms of another thing (often a concrete entity). They offer many examples; for example, 'ARGUMENT IS WAR', 'TIME IS MONEY' and 'LANGUAGE IS A CONDUIT'. The first metaphor gives rise to expressions such as: 'Your claims are indefensible.' 'He attacked my argument.' 'I destroyed his argument.' 'I won the contest.' While they admit the content of concepts may be culture-dependent, it is argued the way we structure them metaphorically is universal.

This approach to meaning is mentalist. But, unlike Saussure's, its focus upon concepts pushes the explanation of language further back, and, for some a worrying development, it suggests that language is grounded in non-linguistic thought. Although not explicitly stated, Lakoff and Johnson seem to argue that language and thought are distinct forms of mental information and that thought is in the driving seat. Figure 23 diagrams this movement away from the overt signals of language. The thick vertical line shows the division between the actual signals of language and the mental sensations of language, the dotted arrowed line represents a gradation from unconscious to conscious mental activity, and the bottom line the assumed movement from concept (general thought category) to sense (specific meaning of acoustic image) to overt signal.

The main objections to conceptual semantics are, one, there is no evidence that concept and language have different locations in the brain, two, common sense suggests they co-exist and three, even if you assume they are separate, there is no evidence for a convergence.

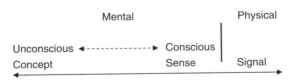

Figure 23 Signal, sense, concept

Summary

Comparing the different views outlined above, we can see two broad positions – internalist and externalist. Although not exactly the same, in philosophy, these positions are termed realist and holist. The former, whether of the direct or indirect kind, tends to be more concerned with the compositional nature of language. It believes the semanticity of language derives from its system. Both Saussure and Chomsky hold internalist views. For Saussure, language was in the mind structuring our thought, a system of checks and balances where the fundamental elements are the relations between the linguistic signs. For Chomsky, it is also in the mind, innately so, and, in contrast to Saussure, its fundamental core is a set of universal logical principles that govern the structuring of all human languages. Although Saussure acknowledged the role of society in fixing the meanings of words through convention, neither he nor Chomsky were interested in examining language's social connections in detail.

With externalist, holistic views the emphasis changes to language use, behaviour and the interactions of communication. Austin, Paul Grice and John Searle would focus upon how language functioned as a tool of communication. The ordinary-language philosophy that their work grew out of was a movement towards the social character of language. It is a return to the notion of speech as a mode of action and a departure from language as a countersign of thought.

Naturally, there are differences among theories that belong to either of these broad divisions. For example, Halliday's systemic grammar may be an externalist theory, but it differs from speech act theory. Whereas the latter treats the speaker as if s/he were an isolated individual performing a set of acts, Halliday has language not as a system of linguistic acts, but 'a system of meanings that defines [. . .] the potential for meaning' (2003: 79). For him, the true significance of speech acts cannot be understood without reference to the social context and its system.

Another division among major thinkers is whether our use of language is totally systematic or not. If it is, it is a conscious rational activity. However, most agree that some operations of language are beyond the ken of our conscious minds. Yet despite the role of the unconscious, both sides argue that we are free to create new meanings, although views differ as to the extent of that freedom. Radical holistic positions which stem from Wittgenstein's later work reject the possibility of a systematic account of language, while moderate positions suggest that only a partial explanation might be possible. They emphasize the dynamic changing nature of language as one of the causes. At the opposite end of the spectrum are realists who argue that all the fundamental problems concerning meaning and understanding can be understood through the analysis of the logical structure of language.

Conclusion

Which theory best describes the nature of meaning? The way language names things or the way the system of language organizes itself? The way intention can change the meaning of an utterance or the way our minds categorize concepts? All of these theories capture important aspects of language and help us towards a greater understanding, yet none of them capture everything. There seems to be only one thing that we can be sure about: there can be no absolute resolution to the question of meaning. It is complex, elusive, and something that is always in the making. Figure 24 makes it clear why this is so.

The line at the bottom indicates that sound, structure and lexicon all contribute to meaning. The lines that descend upon 'meaning' show that every situation is affected by speaker's intentions, beliefs

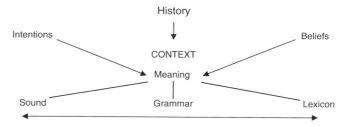

Figure 24 Semantic model of language

and context of utterance. These variables are subtly determined by history, the age we find ourselves in. If among these different contributory aspects only one is chosen, it is bound to distort. We can also sense that their combined effect makes meaning bigger than language. In its primal state, it is amorphous, something that awaits expression. Thought is the force that trawls its depths with the net of language, its every haul shaping and naming. And yet, ever its depths remain.

Chapter 7: *We looked at why semantics has become a difficult subject. Some of the reasons cited were the number of different disciplines interested in meaning, divisions and subdivisions, terminology, and so many different approaches. We then considered four approaches – reference, sense, context and concept. We concluded that it was not necessary to agonize over which theory was more correct, but only to view them as contributions to our fuller understanding. Latterly, we thought that meaning was bigger than language, like something waiting to be brought into the light.*

Study Questions

1. List some of the main differences between spoken and written language.
2. Do you think written language is more exact than spoken? Why? Give some reasons.
3. To what extent do you think context affects meaning? Can you think of any situations where understanding language is determined by context?
4. Can you think of any situations when you have failed to understand what someone meant? Think about the reasons for these communication breakdowns.
5. Why do you think 'truth' enters a discussion of meaning? Do you think meaningful statements have to be 'true'?
6. What implications does the claim that our knowledge of language is unconscious have?

Chapter 8: *In the next chapter, we will look at symbolism.*

From Whence the Power of Symbols?

Introduction

The various approaches to the question of meaning may disagree on its ultimate nature, but all agree that the *method* employed for its linguistic transfer is symbolic. We use the symbolic signs of language to represent the meanings of our thoughts. When we inform others, the signs of thought become the signals of speech.

In this chapter, we begin by making clear what we shall mean by 'symbol'. Not an easy task, because symbolism is so close to the very heart of what it is to be human that there are many definitions. We then proceed to clarify its nature by comparing it to other kinds of signs. Next, we consider its relation to individuals and its role in society so as to better understand its power.

Towards a Definition

Sound plus meaning equals an expression. When that sound is a word, a phrase or a sentence, they become linguistic expressions. These expressions function symbolically by standing for something else. Their role is to represent not just the real, but everything we can conceive. The sound could be silent and heard only by one's mental ear, or it could be shouted above the heads of a crowd. It makes no difference – in both cases, the message is symbolically coded. Figure 25 illustrates the gist of this working definition.

The plus sign represents the link between phonological and conceptual systems, the arrows of the equal sign the 2-way relation of the symbol. Its indirect connection to referents is indicated by

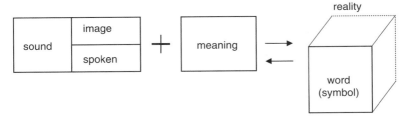

Figure 25 Word plus meaning equals symbol

the faint dotted line. Going in the opposite direction, it has an associative link to the linguistic system to which it belongs.

This is not all there is to the symbol, but, for the moment, let it suffice. From now on, when you read 'sign', 'word', 'phrase' or 'sentence' understand them as examples of symbols. Let's now look at other features that have been singled out as important to the symbol's definition.

Other Features of Symbols

One attribute that philosophers have made a great deal of fuss about is the mediatory role of the symbol and language in general. Whereas sights, sounds, touch, tastes and smell are immediate, the symbol is described as non-immediate because it requires decoding. It lacks the direct contact that our senses have with the world. But, when we are sitting, listening and chatting to a group of friends, how less immediate does this feel? In this medley of sights and sounds, the interpretation of speech is so instantaneous that it feels as immediate as anything else. Speech, as well as understanding, comes as naturally as movement. So, although we may be acting through the agency of language, this non-immediacy is not something that is felt in terms of time or anything else.

The confusion arises partly from the word 'mediate' which makes it seem as if the signs of language insert themselves, like a screen, between us and the true touch of reality. The words 'immediate' and 'non-immediate' also suggest a time difference between the two kinds of experience. The resolution of this mismatch between the description and the actual experience comes from the pen of William James (1842–1910), one of America's greatest philosophers. He argued that this alleged separation arises from an analysis of experience being re-presented as if it were what the subject had felt at the time of the experience (1912: 12–13). The analysis may be correct, but if it is not felt at the time then it is not psychologically real. In this case, the analysis of the indirect relation of word to object, as shown in Figure 21 of the previous chapter, is presented as if it were felt.

Some argue the exact opposite. They say that symbols are directly present in unconscious mental states. If this is so, they are potentially as immediate as sensations. But in this scenario, they are dormant, peripheral to our conscious states, and somehow escape the searchlights of intention. Such symbols could only become important if they were plucked out of darkness and pushed into the full glare of consciousness where intention could get to work and make sense of them. We shall limit our discussion to the kind of symbols that we are cognizant of. These are the sort most normally associated with the use of language.

Another feature concerns the symbol's role. Closely related to the first point, it is said that the symbol's role is to stand for something else. This standing-in-for is another reason for its being described as non-immediate. Originally, this may have arisen from only thinking of the symbol's referential role. Later, and very much thanks to Saussure, it was recognized as also standing in relation to its own kind. Later, we shall see that it is this pointing to other words that separates the symbol from other signs that can only refer outward. It is this belonging to an abstract system that crucially allows thinking to go off-line; that is, to use the shortcuts of conceptual experiences rather than enacting the same experience again and again.

A third factor is that the definition of symbol can also include objects that stand for other things. For example, a wedding ring indicates that the wearer is married, a national flag a particular country, a crucifix Christ's suffering. Although the same function of associative correspondence is at work here, we shall exclude objects from our discussion for the simple reason that they are not linguistic symbols.

A fourth feature assigned to symbols is an inscrutable element. This is because they can connote more than their basic meanings. This view stems from a number of different disciplines. In linguistics, it usually refers to the associations a word has. These can be positive, neutral or negative, and vary from one person to another. For example, words such as 'imperialist', 'socialist', 'hunting', 'organization' and 'sexual' may have different associations for different people. These feelings are at the very limits of a word's semantic territory, far from its defined core meanings. It is where meaning blurs, becomes indeterminate, and coloured by emotion, social attitudes or political agendas.

In cultural anthropology, anthropologists recognize a mystical, irrational aspect to symbolism. They have found that for some people certain words have power, while others are taboo and should never be uttered. Our focus will be on the rational use of symbols. In psychoanalysis, symbols are studied as they appear in dreams and the subconscious. While this serves to remind us of the extent to which symbols have permeated our being, it is likely that these symbols are visual and do not belong to language.

A fifth feature is that symbols developed out of other simpler modes of reference. This is argued by the world-famous psychologist Jean Piaget (1896–1980) who spent his life studying how children formulate concepts. He viewed symbols as representing an evolutionary progression – from icon to index to symbol. We shall consider the differences between these kinds of signs next, but, before doing so, we will end this section with a reminder that symbols are never alone.

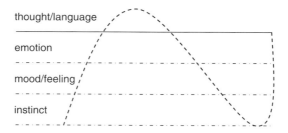

Figure 26 Instinct, emotion, mood, thought/language

Figure 26 is to remind us of the multi-faceted nature of our consciousness. The dotted line that rises from basic instincts through emotional states till it crosses the threshold of the unbroken line into the clearer, more understood, actions of language indicates the movement of our attention. The figure creates the false impression of distinct levels, but even when attention is in the area of language and thought, it is still suffused with mood, feeling and emotion. Words can be uttered with passion or rationally conceived. Nor is thinking always of an intellectual kind. When we try to remember something, it is the job of memory to recall as much as possible in the right order. But memory's mischievous cousin, the imagination, can, if we so will it, arrange events in a different order, one that we might prefer. In other words, thought can be played with.

From Icon to Index to Symbol

It is impossible to say with any certainty whether Piaget's claim that the movement from the icon to the symbol represents an evolutionary progression. But, clearly, there is a gradation from perception to thought – from the relatively easily inferred meanings of visual and auditory signs to the more complicated, shrouded activity of symbolic conceptual activity that we call thinking.

Figure 27 Peirce's triadic action of the sign

To show the differences between the ways these three kinds of signs refer to objects in the world, we will begin with a general outline of Charles Sanders Peirce's ideas. Peirce (1839–1914) more or less invented the subject of **semiotics**, the study of sign systems. His greatest insight was to rephrase the ideas of earlier philosophers on how we associate ideas and things in terms of communication. By doing so, he created a new classification of signs that is relevant to an understanding of language.

Figure 27 shows how Peirce envisaged the relation of the sign's three dimensions to its composite whole. In his theory of signs, he described life as a train of thought, with each semiotic act leaving in its wake a memory. To keep things simple, the Figure does not adopt his difficult terminology.

In Figure 27, we can imagine strings of signs forming semiotic acts that flow through space-time, one part shedding to form memory, the other, propelled forward by energy, to form the next semiotic act.

Figure 28 diagrams the three kinds of relation that Pierce claimed the sign token ('word' in Figure 27) has to the physical object it represents – icon, index and symbol.

Starting from the left of Figure 28, there are the ubiquitous sounds and sights of the world that comprise its appearance. By

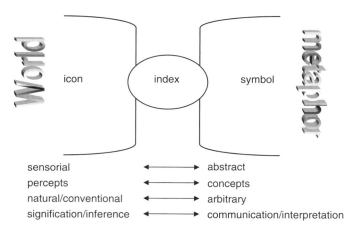

sensorial ⟷ abstract
percepts ⟷ concepts
natural/conventional ⟷ arbitrary
signification/inference ⟷ communication/interpretation

Figure 28　Icon, index and symbol

doing so, they offer themselves up as potential candidates for signs. Once they are named, they become linguistic signs. They are icons if there is a similarity (culturally determined or otherwise) to the objects or state of affairs that they are believed to denote. In the middle, possibly forming a link between icon and symbol are indexical signs, those which have a causal connection to the object they denote, such as shadow to light. On the right, in contrast to the icon, is the non-sensorial symbol – a mental phenomenon that can represent both sensory and abstract data. Once uttered, it becomes sensorial. The vehicle that carries it outward into the public domain is either sound or script. Each symbol is connected arbitrarily to a meaning which is stored in a system of signs called language. The system is stored in the neural networks of the brain and kept in circulation by society. To the far right of the Figure is **metaphor**. Metaphor has both broad and narrow meanings. In its broadest sense, all of language could be thought of as a metaphor – our image of the world as we conceive it. In its narrow sense, it is a figurative use of language. When two, often contrasting, images are juxtaposed – a literary ploy called metaphor – the successful result can be that the listener or reader sees in his or her mind's eye a new image. In this we see a source of creativity: from the fusion of symbolic images irrupt new images. Both sides of the Figure are open because as the world changes language changes and vice versa.

In what follows, we shall draw from Terrence Deacon's wonderfully lucid account of Peirce's far less clear account of his own ideas (Deacon 1997: 47–101). In Peirce's scheme, **icons** were usually of a natural or conventional kind and of a visual or auditory nature. They are mediated, that is brought together, by a similarity between sign and object. For example, photographs and paintings are iconic of what they depict. **Indices** are mediated by some physical or temporal connection. For example, a thermometer indicates a temperature, a weathervane the direction of the wind. The indexical connection depends upon what the person has come to associate the sign's token with. For example, a particular smell may act as an indexical sign to the person noticing it if s/he has always associated it with something else, curry, for example. If, on the other hand, this is the first time the smell has been noticed and it does not indicate anything else, then the interpretation (if it continues), will revert to 'What's that smell similar to?' In other words, it becomes an attempt to forge an iconic link via memory to previous smells. **Symbol** tokens are mediated by some formal or agreed-upon link, irrespective of any physical characteristic of sign and object. This is why their relationship is termed arbitrary: no resemblance to the thing signified is necessary. It is this that enables them to substitute for things and ideas.

Because these terms have been around long before Peirce, they have been used differently by others. In linguistics, iconicity generally only refers to **onomatopoeic** words (words that mimic sounds or actions, e.g., 'wham', 'bang', etc), and indices usually refer to deictic words that make sense in a spatiotemporal context, e.g. 'now', 'there', 'this one', etc. This can create the false impression that certain words belong to one group and others to a different category of sign. But the important point to remember is that no sign is intrinsically an icon, index or symbol. It boils down to how the relation of the sign's token to the actual object is conceived. Is it associated by similarity? If so, it is an iconic sign. Is it contiguity (nearness or connectedness) or correlation (of predictable co-occurrence)? If so, it is indexical. For the symbol, it is law – its formal aspect of behaving according to rules or conventions. This is why some words can be iconic, indexical and symbolic. For example, the word 'cuckoo' exhibits iconicity insofar as it mimics the sound of the bird, but it is also indexical insofar as it will, when heard, spark associations in the mind of the hearer – spring, for example. But when it refers to the bird, as opposed to other birds, the nature of its mediatory role becomes symbolic.

Peirce's classification represents three possible ways in which ideas can be associated. Naturally, language reflects all three. For example, similes are based on an iconic relation – 'as hard as rock', 'like water', etc. **Metonymy** reflects indexical relationships in the way the named part stands for the whole. For example, the 'crown' and 'the White House' stand for, respectively, 'the monarch' and 'the President'. In fact, there is usually some physical contiguity as is the case with indexical associations. Symbolic associations are best illustrated by how words can extend their meaning metaphorically. How, for example, the basic meaning of 'trigger' referring to a part of a gun can be extended to include 'set off', 'begin', as in 'That remark triggered off a disastrous chain of events'.

Peirce also explained the difference between these three kinds of signs in terms of levels of interpretation. He showed how one kind of sign can be substituted for another when the type of associative relationship changes. This is one of the reasons why Deacon believes symbolic reference grew out of iconic and indexical reference. He argues very persuasively that there is a ladder of ascent from icon to index to symbol and that each level depends on the other. For Deacon, the ascent to the symbolic threshold was due to 'a change in mnemonic strategy' (1997: 89). As the number of symbolic signs we used grew, it naturally began to assume the form of a system. At some point, this prompted a realization on the part of its users, an insight, a gestalt. The result was a subsequent shift in how we represent. Instead of searching for associations among physical stimuli of an iconic and indexical kind (of the kind that animals are locked into), we began to use the symbols of an abstract system to stand for those same things and more. This resulted in a radical transformation to our mode of representation. As we became more able to generalize, the representations became more abstract and logical. In short, this represented an advance from percept to concept.

Deacon's explanation usefully highlights the fact that the symbol is not the only kind of sign that has a referential function – so do icons and indices. It also offers us a clearer understanding of how, when the symbol's relation is closer to the inner reality of its own symbolic system, it can seemingly free the activity of thinking from the demands of time and place. This mode is often termed 'off-line' and will be looked at in more detail later.

Summary

The symbol has two essential features. The first is to substitute itself for something else. Its arbitrary nature enables it to do this by belonging, not to the world, but to a system that represents it. The second is the collective agreement of the language community. It marshals this agreement by being available for public use. These are the foundational pillars of language – a potentially free-floating symbol and social use. The latter shapes the meaning of symbols, robbing them of their freedom for the sake of directing action more effectively along, for the most part, the well-trodden paths of everydayness.

Is there Any Kind of Meaning that Does Not Depend on Signs?

Is there any meaning that is not derived from the primordial sign? The German philosopher Immanuel Kant (1724–1804) postulated twelve basic categories of human thought as our a priori tools for making sense of the world. Among them are sensations, emotions, time and space relations, sensing resemblance and difference, quantity, quality, and (more controversially) being able to discern relations of cause and effect. We would know one bird from two, hardness from softness, and that the glimmer of sunrise signalled the onset of day. Kant argued that these are the concepts of **pure reason** (thought that does not depend upon experience), and that they are either presented directly by the schemata of perception, or indirectly by means of the symbol. Those that are presented directly would not derive from acts of **semiosis** (the use of signs). Therefore, certain fundamental relations in the world are understood outside of acts of semiosis. These belong to the innate cognitive apparatus of our species. They fall under the rubric of the anthropologically given, the rest – how we construe and transform the given – is our contribution. And, essentially, it belongs to our use of language.

But does the anthropologically given form any connection to linguistic thought? It must. The presence of an organized nervous system must be of great importance. On this matter, we shall adopt the view that there is continuity between our basic cognitive capacities and linguistic abilities. It is a view amply supported by research findings in both cognitive science and psychology. It suggests that linguistic thought emerged from our prelinguistic cognitive capacities, especially those of perception. Those capacities would have included the ability to sense iconic and indexical signs, the same out of which symbolism may have emerged.

Now that we have described the nature of the symbol, we will turn our attention to its workings within the individual.

The Sign and Individuals

While Figure 27 illustrated the sign and its component parts and Figure 28 its object relations, neither showed that signs only come into existence when they are perceived and, quite literally, have life breathed into them. Figure 29 places signs in relation to the individual, and individuals in relation to social reality via the **sign world**. We use this term rather than, for example, 'social reality', to foreground just how steeped in symbolism our societies are. The sign world holds the collective world of thought.

In Figure 29, there are two humans – Being 1 and Being 2. The linguistic signs of their dialogue are shown by the horizontal, double-headed, arrows. Within the personal spheres of their Being, the signs of their inner dialogues are shown by vertical lines. The meanings of signs that impinge upon their minds but remain unvoiced are shown by single-headed arrows. Signs from the subconscious are shown by black dotted arrows if they are grasped and by v-shaped lines if they are sensed but depart with their meanings undeciphered.

Only two individuals are represented in the Figure, but I would like the reader to imagine millions inhabiting a sign world. The limits of this shared sign world are indicated by the surrounding dotted, black line. Its shape is deliberately non-uniform, and should be thought of as an irregular three-dimensional sphere subject to change with holes perforating those parts of its conceptual surface that have yet to become rigidly conventionalized. The individuals who dwell within the societies of this sign world will conceive of it and its contents differently and in a way that is relative to their experiences and how their cultures represent it.

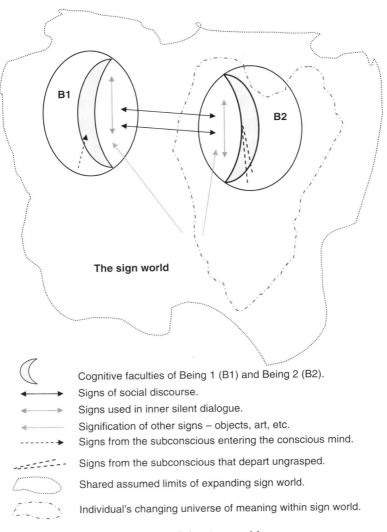

The sign world

☾	Cognitive faculties of Being 1 (B1) and Being 2 (B2).
← →	Signs of social discourse.
← →	Signs used in inner silent dialogue.
←	Signification of other signs – objects, art, etc.
- - - - ►	Signs from the subconscious entering the conscious mind.
~~	Signs from the subconscious that depart ungrasped.
⌒⌒⌒	Shared assumed limits of expanding sign world.
⌒·–·⌒	Individual's changing universe of meaning within sign world.

Figure 29 Signs, individuals, and the sign world

The borders of each individual's knowing will most likely appear less than the sign world's entirety, or in some respect different, since no single individual can know everything that exists in the sign world. This is partly because human beings affect each other's experiences to such an extent that their demands conceal the larger picture. The borders of their knowing are also shown by a faint, dot-dash line which is not closed. In this way, all the signs and paraphernalia of the sign world can flow in and out of their Being, affecting them, just as their personal involvement in the world, subtly affects it.

The sign world owes much of its power to communication technologies – newspapers, television, radio, film, Internet, advertising, etc. – that have caused the presence of language to soar exponentially. Although technology has increased the distribution of information, fundamentally it rests upon our capacity to symbolize, transcribe and finally jettison meaning into space. That space might be public – a billboard, a book, a TV screen, a website, a neon sign, etc. – or private, it hardly matters. What is important is that the overwhelming presence of the sign world has given it such power that many orient themselves by it. Hence, the coining of such words as 'media-driven' to describe societies in which the topics that orientate the interest and lives of their citizens are decided by the media.

To understand the pivotal role played by language in the creation of this sign world, we need to examine language's role in the underlying structure of social reality over which the sign world is draped like a virtual skin.

Symbolization and Social Reality

To show how language has woven itself into the fabric of social reality we shall draw from John Searle's *The Construction of Social Reality* (1995). The reader will recall that Searle was a pioneer in the field of speech act theory. By the time he came to write this book, his attention had shifted to answering something that had puzzled him for a long time: how it could be that there are portions of the world that are only facts by dint of human agreement. Naturally, as a stout defender of the realist position, such a state of affairs would vex him because it makes it appear that 'there are things that exist only because we believe them to exist' (1995: 1). The reader may recall that for realists things are supposed to exist independently of the knower.

Searle begins by separating two kinds of facts. Facts such as governments, money, marriage are termed 'institutional reality'. He contrasts them to 'brute facts' (Mt. Everest, oceans, planets, etc.), the sort that realists like because they need no human institution for their existence. He then claims three factors account for the objective reality of the institutional kind: the assignment of function, collective intentionality and constitutive rules. As we consider his account, we shall see how closely it resembles the way symbolization works.

Searle begins his account by explaining how the capacity of assigning functions to objects – both naturally occurring ones as well as those especially created to perform particular tasks – creates social facts. Thus, the F of X is to Y: the function (F) of this screwdriver (X) is to screw (Y). However, in the case of institutional facts, the formula is different. The function of this $20 bill is to count as money: X (this paper) counts as Y (money) in C (context). In other words, the paper of the bill may not actually be worth $20, but collective agreement assigns the function of this worth to it. This is the crucial element in the creation of institutional facts. Searle calls this kind of function a status function. When such status functions become a matter of general policy, the formula acquires a normative status and becomes a constitutive rule (1995: 48).

The connection between these two factors – assignment of function and collective agreement – and language does not escape

Searle's notice. He argues there is a very special relationship between the imposition of status function and language. Just as the meaning of symbols depend upon conventionalization so, too, do the assignment of status functions. In fact, they are virtually identical. In the same way you do not need a horse present to talk about horses, you do not need real gold or silver to be used as money in current use. This $20 bill will do in the absence of something of that real value. The substitution is more convenient. All that is needed is collective agreement. Every act of language exemplifies this. This is why we do not need to preface every remark with 'let these words stand for'. That agreement is in place.

Searle provides a good example. He asks us to imagine a primitive tribe that initially builds a wall around its territory. This wall marks the boundary of the tribe's territory. The wall fulfils this function by virtue of its height. But, over time, the wall begins to crumble until it is no more than a scarcely visible moss-covered hump. Despite this, the tribe still continue to recognize the humps as marking the boundary. The line now has a function that is not performed in virtue of sheer physics, but in virtue of collective agreement. This state of affairs is symbolic because the remnants of the wall still perform the function of indicating territorial limits. Now, it is no longer because of its height, but because it has been collectively assigned a new status – boundary marker. Searle rightly observes that this seemingly natural and innocent development is 'momentous in its implications' (1995: 40).

Searle remarks that, although anthropologists routinely claim the human capacity for using tools as the radical break with other life forms, the real break comes when, through collective intentionality, humans impose functions on phenomena where the function cannot be achieved solely in virtue of the artefact's structure. These acts require continued human cooperation in the specific forms of recognition, acceptance and acknowledgment of the new functional status. This, he believes, is 'the beginning point of all institutional forms of human culture,' and it must always have the structure X counts as Y in C (1995: 40). We can understand this to mean that culture mirrors the same operations involved in symbolism. That's how integrated symbolism and society are: they grew out of the same seed – agreement regarding substitution on the grounds of practicality.

Synthesis

We shall use Figure 30 to bring together Searle's analysis of the pivotal role of symbolization in the construction of social reality with our own description of the two-way traffic between the signs that are the virtual skin of that reality and the individuals who occupy it.

In this Figure, the strangely shaped tube represents mind. Entering it are sensory data. Before entering, they pass through the

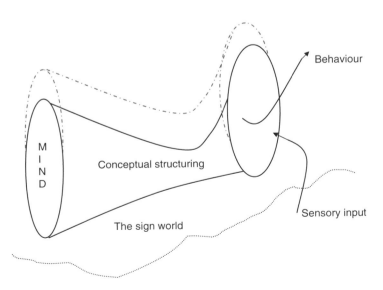

Figure 30 The interface

filter of the sign world represented by the dotted black line. Most often, they reach us as affected in some way, or even as clearly pre-packaged. Once sense is made of the data – whether this involves thinking or passive acceptance – it may result in activity of a mental or physical kind. A large, though unquantifiable, amount of that activity will be linguistic and of a kind that is involved in directing actions to meet needs. Outside of the individual, language (only one part of the apparatus of the sign world) is playing the pivotal role in allowing the functional systems of modern society – monetary, political, social, commercial, etc. – to develop and further organize this kind of purposeful behaviour.

In Searle's analysis, the Background (his technical term for capacities, abilities and general know-how) is not intentional (1992: 175), but there is a Network of intentional phenomena (meanings, understandings, interpretations, beliefs, etc.) that functions against it. His Network of intentional beliefs is part of the Background (1992: 176) and roughly corresponds to our sign world. But, unlike Searle's Network, our sign world is not passive. It is intrusive. Some parts, most obviously messages from advertisers, are deliberately designed to affect our behaviour and thought. Another difference is that in our scheme the assumptions of the Background reside not only in the conceptual architecture of individual minds, but also in the sign world. In fact, the system of interconnections that the sign world forms acts as a conduit along which most of the assumptions held in the Background can travel. It is this movement to and fro the sign world and the individual that causes changes to values and assumptions. The sign world's network of intentions forms a collective world of thought to which each individual not only belongs but cannot escape. Individuals internalize the beliefs held in the sign world through interactions that shape the very nature of their intentionality. In Searle's terms, it makes intentionality 'aspectual' (1992: 156–157). Or, expressed in another way, human intentionality makes it appear that everything in the world is there *for* something.

In the Figure, the dash-dot line that replicates the tubular shape represents the harlequin nature of human consciousness – how through symbolization we can seemingly abstract ourselves from the context of present reality. In this mode, the mind immerses itself in its system of representation ignoring the world outside. For example, one day you are walking in a park admiring the trees. Another day, walking in the same park you are lost in thought, scarcely noticing the fine oaks and beeches of the day before. Thinking to yourself, 'Why did Bill say that?' or 'What phrase should I use?' or 'What's going to happen?' In other words, our attention is focussed less on the outside than it is on the inside. This is not a difference of time, place or person, but of psychic distance between two poles of attention. What shall we call the extremes of those poles? Let's call one inward and the other outward. The former is characterized by working with abstract symbols, the latter with receiving sensory data and, sometimes, transforming them into the symbols of language.

It is possible that we may not have had this capability before our symbolic communication-system developed in tandem with society to a particular level of complexity. But when we do this – look inward, imagine ourselves objectively, or in the future or the past, or think about how others must perceive us – we do not think it unusual. Quite the opposite, it feels natural. Symbolization has, then, provided a means whereby individuals can, through a mental process of abstraction, achieve different modes of Being. In other words, not only do we use words to symbolize something, we can also symbolize ourselves beyond ourselves to bring to bear a different perspective on our selves.

Fundamental to the development of this mode must have been the capacity to take on the role of the other. From a very early age children learn to assume the role of an imaginary other in play – girls playing with dolls imagine they are mother, boys playing with guns imagine they are soldiers. By the time they reach adulthood, people are used to assuming the role of what social theorist George Herbert Mead (1863–1931) described as 'the generalized other'.

When we sympathize we put ourselves imaginatively in someone else's position. Or, conversely, we can imagine ourselves as the object of someone else's interest, and even take a third-person perspective on such an interaction. The result is people soon learn to view situations not just from their own standpoint, but from that of others.

In Figure 30, the ill-perceived limits of the sign world are intimated by the outermost dotted line. This line represents the limit of language and beyond its final border of messages, meanings and mediated reality lies a nameless and, as yet, unnamed reality. A darkness. If a person were taken to an unspoilt and uninhabited island, his or her mind would bring all the paraphernalia that the sign world had already sown and so begin to people that world with meaning. And even if a person were not transported to such a place, but had been born a member of a tribe of an isolated island, history shows that culture arises from human activity. It is our beehive. It is the outcome of collective human behaviour and symbolization is integral to its process. Language is our 'home', our metaphysical environment. This view concurs with Wittgenstein's argument that the self is not 'in' the world, but the limit of it.

Prison or Palace?

The feeling of being trapped in language prompted Jacques Lacan (1901–1981), a psychoanalyst in the structuralist tradition, to write of 'the prison house of language'. Strongly influenced by Saussure, he reinterpreted Sigmund Freud's works, proposing a psychoanalytic model of communication in which the subject was autonomous. The idea was that the subject was locked into the structure of language – a prison from which there was no escape. Language exists and by acquiring it, we enter this prison unwittingly. Instead of Descartes's 'I think, therefore I am', Lacan's refrain was 'It thinks', where it is the Other – the elementary structures of culture and language – that think for us.

It is a gloomy picture and not one that we need to fully subscribe to. We could agree that we are trapped, but given the astronomical chances against life, let alone intelligent life, it would be a lot fairer to say we are in a palace. And besides, to continue the metaphor, the palace has windows that allow newness to enter. Our consciousness does not only reveal to us the degree of our entrapment. Although many of the things we do may be prompted by physiological needs or social obligations, when we know that we could have done otherwise, then we recognize choices and the degree of freedom that we possess. The extent to which language helps us to understand a situation and make choices is the measure of its role in freeing us. This is why Whitehead describes language as 'a bid for freedom' (1927: 65).

Lacan's account also fails to recognize that linguistic signs are only constrained by the conceptualizations that their users wish to entertain. Every great work of literature attests this fact by widening the horizons of our world. Ultimately, it is up to individuals to develop their own linguistic talents and expand the horizons of their experience. This is what writers and poets mean when they speak of the truth of the imagination. Lacan also fails to give full credit to the changes that stem from the interaction between language and culture – no one age is ever the same. New discoveries require new interpretations.

Despite this degree of freedom, no one could fail to notice how powerful the institutional forms of reality have become. We have seen how closely society rests upon language for its very existence, but could there be any other reasons for the success and power of symbolism?

The Power of the Sign World

The French philosopher, Jacques Derrida (1930–2004), examining Husserl's *The Origin of Geometry* on how certain ideas become timeless truths cited two reasons. The first is the persistence and ideality of the written symbol. Writing persists over time. In this lies the strength, not only of institutions, but the whole apparatus of history. Writing is, he stated, 'the condition of the possibility of ideal objects and therefore of scientific objectivity' (1976: 27). In other words, once ideas are transcribed, they take upon themselves an objective existence – they are outside of us. They also survive in written form for a lot longer than the minds that gave them their original expression. The second reason he cited was repetition. He argued that repetition was not a mere repeating of an original meaning, but that it was through repetition that the illusion of presence and self-identity came about and that 'absolute ideality is the correlate of a possibility of indefinite repetition' (1973: 52). Put simply, through sheer repetition and reinterpretation, ideas – some dating as far back as classical Greece – accrue to themselves an apparent immortality. These ideas can range from mathematical truths to simple ideas contained in nursery stories like *Red Riding Hood*. This is why Derrida goes even further than Lacan and declares that humans are not the creators of meaning, but rather inhabit a world created by the impersonal forces of language.

In passing, it is interesting to note the different attitudes towards symbolism. On the one hand, there are no-nonsense types who want the facts and decry symbols as mere make-believes that veil and distort the simple truth. On the other, there are those who see in the symbolic elements of life not a masquerade, but an enhancement of an act. The crowning of the monarch gives an extra significance to the meaning of monarchy. Ironically, the word 'ritual' mirrors these two attitudes. On the one hand, it can refer to a symbolic act, and, on the other, derogatively to an act that lacks any meaning. In this, we see that symbolism can be a source of wonder or illusion. It can heighten our sense of reality or misinform us. It is here we sense the danger of its power.

To return to our main point, it would seem that the invention of scripts did much more than merely guarantee the transmission of culture. It allowed the accumulation of history and this, in its turn, has become a force for the perpetuation of the functional systems (institutional realities) of modern societies. But we know that changes do occur. Society is not bound by symbolism; they evolve symbiotically. While some forms of symbolism may be discarded or fall into disuse, the symbols of language can never be entirely replaced. This is because they are there so that society can function. Language is used to evoke an awareness, sometimes an anxiety, of the basis of common purposes. It does not matter what political creed a state swears by, it needs the symbolism of language to direct the behaviour of its citizens.

Conclusion

We have seen how symbolism has changed us and our societies. But the symbols of language are not the only kind at work. There are others that belong to different media, such as computers and other forms of digital technology. Jean Baudrillard (b. 1929), an anthropologist of modern society, discerns three different orders of simulation. The first is traditional, where the representation attempts to capture the real. For example, television documentaries, landscape paintings, novels, maps and so on. In the second, the distinction between the real and the representation becomes blurred. Fiction is based on fact or facts upon fiction. The third order departs from the symbols of language and its simulations produce a virtual reality. This reality is not measured in terms of how well it represents the real, but in terms of how well it creates new worlds. Baudrillard calls it the 'hyperreal', a world without a 'real' origin. He wonders if this kind of fantasy product will dominate the way we experience the brave new world of the future. Clearly, the symbol, like a key, has unlocked and set in motion a chain of events that are still unfolding.

Chapter 8: *We gave a definition of the symbolic sign and considered features of other definitions. This led into a more detailed discussion of different kinds of signs – icon, index and symbol. The role of symbolism in society was then considered and it was argued that many aspects of our society could not exist without symbolism. It was claimed that script is the site and source of the ideal meanings that not only populate our cultures but also exert a force upon their future directions. Latterly, it became clear that unlike our sensory experiences of the world, we could be mistaken and misled by symbolism.*

1. Think of some symbolism typically found in (a) churches, (b) pop culture and (c) everyday events.
2. Give some examples of symbolic gestures that politicians and other public figures make use of.
3. For those who have read George Orwell's *Animal Farm,* ask yourself which character represents the messenger of the new revolutionary government. Then think of some of the tactics the messenger uses to explain changes to the original manifesto to the workers on the farm.
4. In Orwell's classic *1984*, the totalitarian state attempts to change language. It creates 'double-speak'. Can you think of any recent attempts by governments to use language with a view to manipulating public opinion?

Chapter 9: *The next chapter looks at how language is represented in the mind.*

How Is Language Represented in the Mind?

Introduction

If we could open a head, look in and poke around, would we find words lying in bed with the thoughts that are claimed to awaken them? Of course not. Even though we know where some of the operations of language take place, we are not going to find words. Nor will we find letters scattered about – an 'a' here, a 'z' there, with an 'e', 'b' and 'r' hanging around just in case a conductor should appear and step up onto a rostrum and tap his baton for the word 'zebra'. All we will see is grey matter. Put this nerve tissue under powerful microscopes and we shall see **neurons** (nerve cells), billions of them. This is the physical base of language. Their excitation gives rise to mental representation. The leap from brain to mind, from the physical to the mental, is powered by an electrochemical charge. How that initial firing can kickstart the mind is beyond our present understanding, but it is the subject of intense research and at the very frontiers of scientific enquiry.

In this chapter, we will begin in the basement and relate what is known about the physical foundation of language. Next, we will go up a few floors to the level of mental representation and compare explanations about how the representation of language is thought possible. Then we will consider the notion of representation as indirect mediation. This will lead into a comparison of how two cognitive theories believe that representation may be organized. The stark choice between these rival views that reflect historical divisions between rationalist and empiricist outlooks will spur us to look for another option. Finally, sensing we are at the scientific limits of what language can tell us of how it represents, we conclude.

The Basement

The brain is the most complex object known to us in the universe. John Ratey, clinical professor of psychiatry at Harvard Medical School, writes, 'There are a hundred billion neurons in a single human brain, and roughly ten times as many other cells that have noncomputational roles' (2002: 9). These neurons are connected to each other by branching, tree-like connections called axons and dendrites which terminate in tiny structures called synapses. Ratey writes, 'Each one of our hundred billion neurons may have anywhere from 1 to 10,000 synaptic connections to other neurons' (2002: 9). This means that, theoretically, the number of different, possible patterns of connections in a single brain is roughly 40,000,000,000,000,000. Forty quadrillion. The synapses do not actually meet. There is a tiny gap between them across which electrical signals pass and are transformed into chemical ones. These chemical messengers are called neurotransmitters and contain, among other substances, serotonin and dopamine. This leap across extra-cellular space transforms the signal energy and constitutes our psychoactivity. Ratey writes, 'If changes in synaptic strengths [. . .] are the primary mechanism behind each brain's ability to represent the world, and if each synapse has, say, ten different strengths, then the different electrochemical configurations in a single brain come to a staggering number: ten to the trillionth power' (2002: 11). Easily enough to represent a language.

Ratey's account continues with more mind-boggling revelations, but the only point we need to note is that, if we are to avoid mystical or religious explanations, we have to accept that mental representations arise from this electrochemical activity. Because

Ratey's account is not directly concerned with how the brain could give rise to linguistic representations, we shall turn to one that is.

William Calvin, a theoretical neurophysiologist, is actually searching for the mechanism behind all representations, including language. The first thing he does is explain the properties he believes the thing he is looking for will have. Among many other capacities, it has to be able to copy and not so perfectly that it does not make small mistakes when it does so or when it sends information to other parts of the brain. He calls it a Darwinian machine and posits it in the **cortico-cortex** (the outer layer of the brain which has a depth of about 2mm.). It is not in one place, but permeates the entire cortico-cortex. This is where, he believes, representation takes place. If we could see it, he says the surface of our brains would look like a constantly changing patchwork quilt. In order to explain it, he asks us to imagine hexagonal mosaics of electrical activity competing for territory in the association cortex of the brain. It is the pattern within each hexagon that may be the representation of an item of vocabulary, objects, actions, tunes or images. When it is excited, either in response to external stimuli or to internal impulses, the firing deciphers the cerebral code into a word or mental image. He believes there must be a code, a condensed short-form, otherwise how else could memory exist. He describes the hexagon as the smallest unit of an assembly of cells that forms a macrocolumn containing about 100 mini-columns involving about 10,000 neurons. The firing converts the code from its short-form cerebral pattern to its muscular implementation. The pattern of the firing will represent different concepts, words or images. The problem is how to see it, how to capture its millionth of a second existence so as to compare it to others.

It will be remembered that earlier we wrote that Darwinian processes of natural selection took millennia to shape up the various species we see in the world today. However, when the human immune system was found to be capable of creating new antibodies to combat unwelcome antigens in a matter of days-to-weeks, it threw new light on Darwinian processes. It showed that at the molecular level cell mutation is rapid. Calvin wonders if the brain could mimic this creative process using even faster neural mechanisms.

The immensity of the task facing researchers is clear. First, they want to find out how new short-term working memory patterns become encoded and stored in long-term memory. In effect, how the code is formed. Eventually, they want to differentiate between firing patterns – which are for images, which for language? The problem is one of observation. At present, the most advanced medical imaging technology shows where some working memory patterns are located by indicating electrical activity. But copying has not yet been observed. As technology improves, researchers hope to 'see' which fleeting patterns could stand for particular sounds, ideas, images or actions. Any major breakthrough is going to revolutionize the way we think of ourselves.

Up to Consciousness

Perhaps, like me, the reader is wondering where we are among all this pulsing electrochemical activity. Where's Liz, Johnny, little Tommy and my darling Lowenna? We can't feel ourselves, let alone see anyone else in the basement. So let's leave its amazing machinery whirring away and take the elevator up to a floor where the lights of cognition can blaze anew or bask in recognition.

Mental Representations

Well, we've gone up quite a few floors. There were some for the non-conscious operations of the body, like breathing and the heart's pumping of blood. Then there were some dimly lit floors for unconscious habits, like biting nails and lighting up another one. Then, finally, flickering lights were behind us, and we could step out conscious of the world around us. Despite finding it difficult to shake off a nagging feeling that we don't know half of what's going on inside ourselves, let's look at some explanations about mental representations.

Basically, there are three kinds of representation in the mind: images, movement and language. The first is like a picture; for example, when we imagine a tropical beach with coconut trees swaying in the breeze. The second pictures movement. Language's representing medium is very different: it is not images, but sound. And not just any kind of sound, these sounds have to be meaningful. It is this connection to meaning that marks the starting point for how traditional theories explain linguistic representation.

Traditional Representative Theories

Traditional theories believe that the power of words is conferred upon them by our thoughts. These thoughts, ideas, concepts, schema are conceived of as an intermediary medium that lies between perception and language. We shall call this halfway house thought, and let this single word do for ideas, concepts, schema and any others. Clearly, this view speaks for the classical philosophical separation of thought and language. The intermediary medium effects the separation and empowers sound with meaning. The intermediary medium may be a halfway house, but it must not become a relay station to more distant, ever deeper, phenomena that claim to explain its power. In other words, interpretation must stop with thought and go no further.

To rephrase the argument: we understand the sounds of language by associating them with the intermediary medium. So, when we speak, this home medium projects significance onto words, and, when we hear, it maps the sounds onto itself. Put simply, words are explained by their link to thought. And it is the power of thought that explains the significance of words. Hence the claim that thought is primary and language secondary because it is derived.

According to contemporary philosopher Simon Blackburn, the thinking behind this argument goes something like this:

(i)   The link between words and the things they name is arbitrary and springs from conventions. So the power of meaning cannot be in the words themselves. We could, if we chose to, use words to mean different things, or use them stupidly so that no one could understand us.

(ii) If words cannot be signs of nothing, they must be signs of something we *know*. We have to know what they signify before we can understand them. And since what we know is all in the mind, thought must precede speech. It must be our knowledge or beliefs that determine how we understand words.

(iii) *Knowing what* words signify in our minds must mean that we *represent* what they signify in the mind (Blackburn 1984: 44). A further proof of this is that when we use words, we use them simultaneously about the thought we have in our minds. Thoughts, then, are more important than language because they precede it. Thought reigns supreme.

Blackburn cites a number of weak points in this argument. In the first point, why wasn't the power of meaning attributed to the force of social convention? He believes the force of philosophical tradition pushed the argument in the direction of the second point, the power of mind. We shall return to this point later, but note in passing that it is not unusual for philosophers to become so preoccupied with thought that they forget the world around them. The third step in this argument is the one he singles out as most suspect. While most of us would agree that interpreting and translating involves a making sense of something by referring it back to a home medium (what we know, our experience of the matter), does this necessarily entail representation? He suggests it is more likely to be a re-presentation of something we have learnt. He thinks the word 'representation' smacks too much of visual, mental imagery that would be insufficient to represent the world. He rightly points out that when representation is interpreted as re-presentation, it highlights the role of memory in recalling what is known. Let's add some more points to Blackburn's.

First, if, as stated in the third point, we use words simultaneously about the thought, this strongly suggests that they co-exist and that you cannot have one without the other. The way our language is structured does not help us to see this unity, however. It always seems to suggest the opposite. Phrases such as 'language is the tool of thought' or 'thought shapes our language' abound. Some writers claim that a flash in the mind is thought. But can you call anything a thought before it has expressed something? If the flash remained unexpressed, it would be worthless. It would remain a, 'I thought I had it, but it's gone'. Thoughts have to find expression before they can properly fulfil their definition of holding an idea. The flash may be the force of the irruption of thought but it is incomplete. The second point concerns the claim that thought injects meaning into words. Here we have the three witches again – thought, meaning and language. They need to be clarified. In the abbreviated account given above, they are not. Our account has meaning constructed through thinking in language. A clearer definition of 'thought' is badly needed, because the more it sinks into the unconscious the further it departs from its normal sense of 'knowing'. The third point again concerns language. The word 'thought' has strong connections to 'knowledge', and, although 'knowledge' includes beliefs and a wide range of social capabilities, it is often understood as only referring to the intellect. How would it be if we substituted 'experience' for 'knowledge' in this argument? After all, its meanings include such senses as 'knowledge of past events' and 'practical knowledge'. The reason 'experience' is not used is because it has come to be defined as knowledge gained from external events. And yet couldn't the activity of 'thought' be construed as a kind of experience? An experience that remembers another one could represent it as easily as thought could. The point we are making here is that we have stumbled into a semantic minefield. If writers are not to become hopelessly lost in vagueness, these common words must be clearly distinguished from one another. And, even worse, we sense that the way certain words have come to be defined are exerting an influence by pushing the explanation in a particular direction. As to what that direction may be, we will return to that later. The fourth point brings us to a clarification of the meaning of 'represent'. This warrants a section to itself.

The Meaning of 'Represent'

There seem to be three kinds of representation regarding language in the mind. The first concerns the representation of sensory data. For example, when we say, 'That hurt', it describes the hardness of a knock, or, when we say, 'What a stink' to abhor a smell. In this kind of representation, external stimuli are acting in cohort with internal impulses to produce a reaction, often a reflex, which may be reported upon in language. The second kind of representing is when we recall something. As Blackburn noted, we call upon memory to re-present some event or idea to the mind, to bring something back to the present. With this kind, it seems more exact to think of 'representation' as remembering. It does not necessarily involve external sensory data, but rather an awakening of data that has been stored in memory. As to what can spark a memory, the reader will recall the three main links are iconic, indexical and symbolic. The third kind of representation may rely just as much upon memory, but its aim is different. It is not trying to recall the details of the past as accurately as possible, but to construct something new out of past experience. When we rearrange ideas held in language, or other symbolic representational systems, to construct something novel, we are involved in a creative process. On these occasions, we are re-structuring something that is held latently in a representational system – language or the notations of mathematics or music. How shall we interpret 'representation' in these cases? In this case, 'representation' comes closer to 'reinterpretation'. Sensory data is not necessarily involved, nor is exact recall the only objective. In this kind of representation, language is the playground in which novel ideas can be found when intention motivates the search to uncover them.

Let's now consider the main contender to the traditional theory on mental representation.

Another Representative Theory

You will remember that one weak point of the traditional argument was that it pushed the source of the meaning of words in the direction of mind. Ludwig Wittgenstein seized upon this weakness and pursued it to its logical conclusions. In doing so, he laid the foundations for the main rival to traditional representative theories – language as use.

Wittgenstein was not addressing representative theory directly, but the Cartesian notion that we could not be more certain of anything other than our own thoughts. This notion figures in representative theory by lending force to the view that everything begins with thought. Descartes wanted to show that those who claimed we could know nothing for certain were wrong. He did this by trying to prove the certainty we have for our own thoughts. This became known as first-person authority. Wittgenstein attacked this theory of knowledge. First, he showed that we did not need to answer the assumption that objective certainty was necessary to prove everything. Then he attacked first-person authority with a theory of meaning. He did this by showing that the thinker's thoughts were not as isolated from the world as Descartes thought. He argued that the logic of first-person avowals was a by-product of public language and, therefore, could not be used as either proof of an 'inner' private realm or as a blueprint for some supposedly 'private' language. This was because the rules of language that the thinker is using come from the speech community. These rules were not viewed as innate or essentially logical in nature, but **contingent**. In philosophy, this word forms a contrast to **necessary**. The former paints a relative, changing, pluralistic universe explained by experience. The latter paints a priori, absolute, unchanging unity beneath the surface of appearances which cannot be explained by experience. For Wittgenstein, all the rules and conventions of practice were contingent. He argued that we can support our choice of language by appeal to rules and that rules only exist within a practice. Objectivity is a part of the practice, not a way to ground or support its entire edifice. One of the analogies he used to get his argument across was how we get to know and find our way around the streets of a city. In short, he showed the extent to which private thought depended upon public knowledge.

Summary

From the above, we can see that we have representative theories that have thought governing language and, not its exact opposite, social theories that have meaning derived from public practice. A mental view ranged against a social view. Although the social view moves the source of the power of the representing medium out of the individual's mind and into the public domain of social practices, it still has its operations going on inside the heads of individuals. But it weakens the intermediary role of thought by making its container (language) and content (ideas) public and observable. Individuals are no longer kings sitting upon solitary thrones of thought issuing edicts of truth. Instead, they are mere nodes in a social matrix of directly shared thought and action.

By showing that a good deal of thought amounts to following accepted practices, Wittgenstein shifted not only its source, but also undermined its originality. He did this by pointing to the social arena in which thought takes place. This, in turn, underscored the importance of the knowledge discourse each age inherits. Two examples will suffice to show this. In the scientific community, Kepler's three 'laws' about planetary orbits posed the problem that Newton would solve. But Newton's theory involved influences that were transmitted over vast distances instantaneously. This impossibility posed the problem that Einstein would solve. In this, we see how even mathematics, the favourite candidate for transcendental status among rationalists, is grounded in a discourse. The same was equally true of Descartes' ideas. His argument was intended to roll back the tide of scepticism. Scepticism was a school of thought that doubted there could be any absolute certainty about knowledge. Descartes found this view repugnant because he was a devout son of the Catholic Church. He was reacting to certain modern thinkers such as Michel de Montaigne (1533–1592) whose sceptical views were fuelling religious doubt and Pierre Charron's (1541–1603) negative argument for faith. This led him to search for an absolute conception of reality, the very same that centuries later Wittgenstein would undermine. But it is not just the famous who are enmeshed in an inherited discourse, we all are.

The next question we will consider is if it is correct to think of the mediation of representation as a separation. This view pervades much of the literature. Here is an example:

To represent something symbolically, as we do when we speak or write, is somehow to capture it, thus making it one's own. But with this approximation comes the realization that we have denied the immediacy of reality and that in creating a substitute we have but spun another thread in the web of our grand illusion. (Pagel qtd. in Calvin 1996: 172)

How Close to Reality Are We?

There seems to be no alternative to the fact that, when we are thinking, the mind is representing, in the sense of 'substituting' or 'presenting'. But many writers think this substitution amounts to a separation from the touch of reality. Certainly, the word suggests that we are not dealing with the 'real thing'. But just how real is this alleged separation? If, at the time of an experience, no indirectness is felt, then psychologically it cannot count as real. Let's imagine the following kind of experience: someone is thinking. Is this activity any less connected to present reality than someone playing soccer? Surely the thinker and the thought are as much *in* the experience as the player and his or her intention towards the game. And this must apply to any other activity. So how does this notion of separation arise?

It seems to stem from two main causes. The first arises from presenting the analysis of an earlier experience as actually replicating the experience it describes. Just as we know that a chair is composed of atoms but don't experience it, so, too, with this retrospective explanation. The analysis might be true at one level of explanation, but if the separation was not felt at the time of the experience then the analysis cannot be applied at an ontological level. The second reason stems from the fact that certain experiences are stronger, more vibrant, more 'real' than others. Conceptual experiences are often considered less strong, vibrant, and so less 'real'. But can we then describe them as indirect?

Our interpretation, as developed in previous chapters, is that people can, by a shift of attention, move along a continuum of cognition from awareness of the outside to a mental interior. Unfortunately, the sensations of the former and the reasoning of the latter have been fashioned in a way that presents two different views of reality. In this view, they are coordinates of cognition. Percepts at one end, concepts at the other. They are not two distinct forms of cognition. One of the few modern philosophers who saw this point clearly was William James. He put it like this, 'Both thing and thought are the stuff of experience' (1912: 122). Some experiences lead the agent in one direction – towards the thing – others lead in another direction – towards the mental. We can be lost in thought, have our head in the clouds, be daydreaming, but we are still in the here-and-now. Abstract thinking, however separate and different it may feel, represents (= typifies) one kind of a range of experiences we are capable of and not an indirect kind of reality. Unfortunately, the habit of speaking as if one reality can be in two places at once has become so ingrained that many write as if every moment is simultaneously lived as both felt and 'thought-about'. If it were, it would be a pathological condition.

Let's now consider how two cognitive theories differ on the question of how language might be organized in the brain.

How Might Language Be Organized?

The two main answers to this question come from theories that belong to a discipline called **cognitive science**. This relatively new discipline is described as 'an interdisciplinary research cluster' by Robert Audi (1999: 148). Its aim is to account for intelligent activity shown by either living organisms or machines. Cognitive psychology and Artificial Intelligence form its core, but at the fringes there is input from linguistics and neuroscience. The first theory we shall call the 'language of thought' hypothesis. The second is called connectionism. Let's consider them in that order.

The 'language of thought' hypothesis was first expounded in 1975 by Jerry Fodor (b. 1935), a philosopher of psychology, in a book of that title. Briefly, he proposed a cognitive architecture in which thought, like language, exhibits productivity. The nature of this productivity has three facets. The first assumes that the mind possesses an innate capacity for storing and manipulating symbols. The manipulation involves syntactic rules which operate in a computational manner. 'Computational' means that the operations are automatic and beyond the reach of consciousness. The second facet is that this cognitive architecture is modular. The third is that virtually all concepts are innate. It is a view that the reader will recognize as owing a great deal to the influence of Chomsky. In its modern sense, 'innate' means 'genetic', and it is argued that the rules and concepts of thought that fuel language are stored genetically.

The inspiration behind this theory comes from computer processing. Fodor believes the system that underlies mental representations resembles the 'machine language' of a computer, while what is present to consciousness is like the computer's visual display. The computer effects all the transformations between the two levels with many 'states' in between. The main focus of research is on linguistic representation and particularly how complex sentences are built up compositionally from smaller components. Computer programs have been constructed to show how we might construct sentences with the belief that their organization reflects structure-dependent rules.

Soon the theory began to attract criticism. Some began to ask why it was so focussed on syntax and nothing else. Why did it exclude the outside world from its consideration? Its critics argued that cognition is much more dynamic and situated in real-world tasks with environmental contexts. Fodor responded by acknowledging that there was an external contribution to the meanings found in cognition, but stated his preference for concentrating on an internal explanation. Probably, he shared the same passion for the formal propositional content of language as Chomsky. The claim that concepts were innate was the reason given for not having to attend to external influences.

The other main theory is **connectionism**. Pioneered by researchers Frank Rosenblatt and Oliver Selfridge, its popularity waned during the seventies but experienced a revival during the eighties as computer technology improved. The connectionist theory, sometimes called **neural network modelling**, attempts to model the way our neurons and their connections work. The system consists of a set of processing units that are assigned activation values. These units are connected so that particular units can excite or inhibit others. Input can come from outside or from the impulses of the units that comprise the system. There are a variety of different architectures and some have created a learning ability. The learning tasks involve pattern-recognition. Their systems have been enabled to learn by 'adjusting the weights connecting the various units of the system' (Audi 1999: 175). This sounds like the way we learn at a neural level. Ratey writes, 'The more firing that occurs across a specific connection [of synapses] the stronger that pathway becomes' (2002: 21). This forms part of his argument that proper stimulation is needed to learn or get better at something. It is not just a case of 'use it or lose it', but 'the more you practise, the better you get'. These networks are also good at modelling cognitive tasks in which there are multiple constraints which have to be observed. However, the networks can override constraints when it is not possible to satisfy all of them. This is interpreted as a form of reasoning. In this theory, the form the rules take are associative links.

Naturally, connectionism also has its critics. Fodor has criticized it on the grounds that the nets do not really match the architecture of the human cognitive system. Connectionist researchers respond by emphasizing the importance of pattern-recognition which Fodor's computer systems have not yet modelled, and by continuing to design more complex networks.

Summary

The differences between the two theories can be summarized as follows. The language of thought hypothesis has innate concepts and categories manipulated by automatic rules operating at an unconscious level with the focus on syntax. Connectionism chooses prototype structures (exemplars) rather than concepts and categories. These prototypes are viewed as less stable and more social than innate concepts that are immune to change. It is not as concerned with syntactic arrangement, but tries to model specific cognitive tasks such as perception, attention and learning. It forms closer connections with associations forming habits. In fact, Audi calls connectionism the 'modern descendant of associationism' (1999: 152).

The main objection to the language of thought hypothesis is its strong claims for innateness. It is generally recognized that while weaker claims are acceptable, strong ones are indefensible. Blackburn rightly wonders how something physical, such as genetic material, could hold concepts and categories in advance of their knowledge (1984: 56–57). We know that concepts change. There is evidence. Technological advances are the material realizations of scientific concepts. But there are also examples of how concepts that have no material expression can change. Guthrie, a historian of philosophy, writing of Parmenides, an early philosopher, cites how, among many other concepts, those of 'kinesis' and the 'infinite' began to develop and change (1965: 37, 46).

However, the modern argument for innateness is more subtle than many credit it. The reader will recall the basic categories of thought that Kant claimed were a priori mentioned in an earlier chapter. Fodor, as well as Chomsky, argue that the organic mental structure of the brain that holds these basic elements of thought also has a module for the language capacity. Fodor argues that this module has the capacity to hypothesize the correct rules of meaning for whatever knowledge exists. It is still a view that requires a previous ability to learn something, but it is more subtle. Hereafter, when we use the word 'thought' in the context of this theory it will refer to this substrata of automatic elements of thought. This is the holy ground for those who argue for innateness.

With the second theory, we find the very idea that Chomskyans believed they had routed back in the seventies returning. Instead of a hierarchy of structure-dependent rules operating automatically under the control of innate mechanisms, we have networks of associations reflecting exposure to repeated experience. The nature of the associations that can be formed must be linked to our innate dispositions, but, in this argument, it is the awakening hand of experience that is given most credit. Henceforth, in the context of this theory, 'experience' will mean external processes which influence the mind by way of habits and association.

This view believes that habits shape neural networks. If you do something frequently enough, it forms an association, becomes 'learnt'. Once it becomes so learnt that it no longer requires any attention, it is a habit. Habits have a physical base in the brain. They can have this physical base because the nerve tissue of the brain is soft and malleable. Currents, whether of blood or electrochemical impulses, will leave their traces in the paths they take. Just as muscles shape themselves to particular exercises, so, too, does the delicate nerve tissue of the brain to repeated sensations. These paths represent a reflex discharge. Naturally, the pathways of complex habits will be more convoluted, one reflex triggering others. In this, we see that the connectionist view is not so different to those of Skinner and other behaviourist psychologists of half a century earlier. The organization of representation takes the form of associative links. Hierarchies are not needed because there are billions of neurons with different groups assigned to different patterns of sensation. Some may shortcut certain links; perhaps, these can be called 'rules'.

It would be unreasonable to expect either view to explain everything since research is still at the very beginning. Naturally, connectionism does not take into account experiences that go unnoticed. It only simulates those that come from the outside of the sort that form impressions on the mind. Accidental variations of the kind that can produce the sensitive hearing of a great musician are not a part of their research program. Nonetheless, the kind of passively received experience that they are simulating accounts for an enormous part of our behaviour. The language of thought hypothesis ignores the knowledge we gain from experience and emphasizes the importance of innate structures. But even if we accept that there is a native wealth of innate knowledge, it does not resemble reality. It applies to it, but has nothing to do with the facts until the facts appear. In other words, these innate truths need real truths. Without the real world, they would be worthless, and we would not know if the properties claimed for this a priori body of truth were true or not. In the case of this particular theory, our senses cannot corroborate the claims it makes because they take place in the unconscious. By its own making, the theory must remain an unverifiable hypothesis.

And so we seem to have come full circle: a just point at which to pause and wonder if there is any other explanation. There is, but before outlining it we need to do a little housekeeping.

Interpreting the Interpretations

Language represents our resources for explanation. On an everyday basis, there does not seem to be much of a problem. But when we probe deeper and try to explain complex phenomena such as what makes mental linguistic representation possible, words begin to wobble. However carefully we choose them, they don't feel as safe anymore. Some come laden with presuppositions, and others, for all we know, with misconceptions. We mentioned earlier an uneasy feeling that we were being led by the way certain fundamental words had been defined. Most of our philosophical terminology comes from ancient Greece. This means it has reached us through numerous translations with countless interpretations appended. A haze surrounds fundamental terms. We have already mentioned a few – 'thought', 'knowledge', 'experience'. The definition of these terms as well as others is signposting us towards a choice which is not of our making, but history's. When we look at many of the keywords we have encountered so far, we see that they fall into two groups. Here, they have been arrayed in two columns in an order that the reader might find familiar.

A	B
internalist	externalist
[systematic, rule] formal	functional [use, relational]
[static, absolute, abstract] rule	convention [practice, habit, process]
[not from outside] non-sensory	sensory [from outside]
[universals] whole	part [particulars]
[logic, mathematics] pure science	natural science [observation, experiment]
[natural, genetic] innate	social [nurture, environmental]
[inner, mental] subjective	objective [outer, physical, neutral]
[ideal, knowledge] thought	thing [object, events, real, appearance]
[necessary, intelligible] reason	experience [sensible, contingent]
[immaterial, reason] rationalist	empirical [fact, material]

The words in parentheses are either associated with the word outside or roughly synonymous. Of course, there are more keywords than these, and some of the combinations may be dubious. But the aim of the list is to indicate the nature of the discourse we have inherited, not to explain it. Clearly, it shows a division.

Historically, the division is rooted in the separation of 'thought' and 'thing', the cornerstone of Platonism. Circling this fateful division are many reflections: inner–outer, mental–material, ideal–real, subjective–objective, life–matter, etc. It is a division that has radically affected our perception of the world. If you doubt this, ask yourself how it must have been to have lived in an age before the separation of life and matter – at a time when people saw all matter as animate to some degree – to have watched the movement of the sea as if it were a living body, the wind stirring a field as if a hand were crossing it, and mists rising as if they were spirits. And, inwardly, people asking themselves if they had angered the gods or whether they should offer a cock to Zeus to gain favour. That view of the world began to erode as more and more order was observed in nature, first by religions and then by science. Order strongly suggested design. Design the existence of mind. The sheer scale of the cosmic order meant it had to be a divine mind. Gradually, the cause and origin of that order was wrested from the divine by science offering successful explanations only in terms of nature. But the legacy of this classical division persists and we are still caught in its crossfire.

Looking down the list we see that these words reflect two different views of knowledge. Those in column A are often used to express the desire of the formalist of a rationalist persuasion for absolute rules. To be absolute and unchanging, these rules need to be tucked away in a safe place, such as an ideal realm or in the fastnesses of innateness. The key aspects of the order they seek are that it should be a unity and immutable. The words in column B often express the belief of the empirically minded: whatever order there is, is the outcome of chance and, not only has the world evolved, it is still evolving. Between the two positions there are points in common. For example, most rationalists accept Darwinism, but some seem reluctant to let go of the notion of design behind the universe's course of development. And, naturally, empiricists also recognize order, laws of nature underlying and explaining some of the appearances of the world. But they refuse to believe in forms and forces either transcendental or inherent actively organizing this order.

The effect of the legacy has been to create a contest between the two schools of thought which sometimes seems more intent on defending positions than presenting the entire truth. Another effect has been to sculpt out paths in our language that lead inevitably, if you follow the signposts of definitions, to the same stark choice. One can only wonder what other meanings might have populated our language had a different proposition gained more importance than Plato's. The positions also seem to reflect two basic psychological types: those that love everything to be neat and tidy and their opposites who are content to live with organized chaos.

Is there any way out of the crossfire? Is there no other option?

Pure Experience

There is. If you believe, as James argued, that 'thing' and 'thought' are the stuff of experience, they merge into one. They become coterminous and the usual discontinuity that is argued for between the knower and the known vanishes. If you accept this redefinition of 'experience' as including mental activity, then most of the key-words collapse into one experience. The known and the knower, object and subject, the represented and the representer, inner and outer, sensation and sense-data. Their sheer, utter dependence on one another brings them seamlessly together in the instant field of the present. Their separation is revealed as an analysis after the event. You will be saying: you cannot sever thoughts from the world in which they originated, inhabit and apply to. Most people believe that even those innate categories of thought evolved by processes of natural selection from among the general experience of the species for life on Earth. The function (= role) of consciousness is to alert us to the presence of reality. Cognition is, then, a two-way dependency, saying 'you are in a world'. Our thoughts are a part of the function of cognition, not an escape route to an indirect form of living and a claim for its greater truth. So we can stop trying to remove the one thing that you can never get rid of – reality. Because, if we ever succeeded, there would be no more thought.

But does James's radical empiricism offer us more than just a way out of the wrangling of the two schools? Does it also say something more than the other representative theories about, one, how we manage to make mental linguistic representations, and, two, how those representations might be organized? It does not address the second point, but it does offer a new perspective on the first. If thinking (conceptual experiences is James's phrase) is as direct as sensory experiences, then there is no gap, no need for an intermediary. If thinking is as direct in its relation to the present as anything else, then representation is ongoing. But again, the reader may be wondering, how can thinking which goes on in language, using symbols that substitute for reality, be direct? In other words, surely substitution equates with indirectness. This will only happen if you forget that our stream of consciousness is always directly lived. If you start trying to rationalize experience by talking 'about' it, it begins to seem like a different experience. But the *use* of substituting symbols is as directly present as anything else.

Summary

To recap: we have three views on language's mental representation. The traditional theory is the one most typically presented in linguistics. It argues that representation is indirect and places thought as an intermediary into the gap it creates. The second view is the one often preferred by sociolinguists. Wittgenstein's ideas dethrone thought by situating thinkers as doers in a matrix of language rules and conventions. The two cognitive theories reflect the same divide. The language of thought hypothesis has thought in the driving seat just like the traditional representative theory. Connectionism has more in common with the social dimension of meaning. The third position, briefly outlined above, argues for direct cognition. It claims that traditional theories violate our sense of reality by creating an artificial conception of the relation between the knower and the known.

The main issue remains: are thought and language separate or not? If they are, then representation is indirect. If they are not, and no other gap is discovered or dreamt up, then representation is direct. If it is direct, the presence of language becomes crucial. In all the sad cases of children deprived of speech, there was only one thing they had in common: they did not speak. Only after they were rescued and had love and care lavished upon them, did they begin to. Clearly, there is a strong connection between something being 'present' and its 'representation'. Perhaps the mind reflects whatever is presented to it within the range of its cognitive capabilities. First reflecting, then selecting from among present and past presentations of both inner and outer kinds. If this is the case, there is not much hope of language being able to explain how it does this mirroring.

The Mirror Can't Mirror Itself

In his early work, Wittgenstein argued that language is like a picture. It is a picture of the world made up of words. Just like the pixels that make up the images on your computer screen, words form representations. We use language to mirror the world, explain our inner feelings and even to show logical relations. But the one thing we cannot make it do is mirror itself. It can't show us how it does the mirroring. The mirror cannot mirror what it is about itself that does the mirroring. This is precisely why computers are being used to simulate cognition. Language can represent anything in reality except what it has in common with that part of reality which makes it possible for it to represent it. That part of reality is cognition. Cognition tells us we are in a place, informs our minds we are in a world. Language reports on that fact and much else, but it cannot get outside of cognition. If we could turn language off, like a computer, we would still not be able to examine it. It only has substance when it is representing. Once it ceases to represent, it vanishes. At this point, we discover that the limits of our understanding are the limits of language because understanding takes place within language. And it is at this point that a scientific explanation of language comes grinding to a halt because we cannot get outside of cognition.

Our cognition represents reality perceptually, qualitatively, quantitatively, causally and conceptually. Only if you think that concepts, or certain fundamental concepts, are separate from reality, can you believe we can use language objectively about cognition. This would make it appear that there is a neutral ground, an objective point, from which thought can operate. But nearly all the great thinkers of the past have agreed upon one thing: you cannot rationalize cognition because you cannot get outside of it. If you think language can, then you disagree. If you think it can't, then you agree that our metaphysical space is earthed. And if this is the case, we have reached the scientific limits of the use of language for description.

This in no way discredits the worthy path of science, but as far as explaining how it represents, language is a non-starter. It is a part of that which simply is. Not until we know more about the physical electrochemical foundations of language or develop artificial intelligence or break out of the stalemate of traditional thinking will we be able to say more. But this is not to say our effort has been in vain. By bringing words up against their own walls, we begin to sense the unnamed on the other side.

Conclusion

We seem to have reached the end of our journey. Although this marks a conclusion to a work, it is not, of course, an end to the study of language. It is doubtful if there could ever be a conclusion to such an immensely complicated subject. In that greater enterprise, it is merely a staging post and one which, although appearing to have covered a great distance, has merely brought us back to the beginning, to where we stood at the outset. Hopefully, the ground around us is clearer, less cluttered, and the paths ahead more visible. It is as the poet T. S. Eliot expressed it, we are forever, 'In the ground of our beseeching' (From 'Little Gidding' of *The Four Quartets)*. In this picture, that 'ground' is our Being and our 'beseeching' the quest for authentic meaning.

Further Reading

Chapter 1: What Are the Origins of Language?

On the vocal tract and the uniqueness of human language, Larry Trask's first chapter (1999) is an informative read. For a brief outline of Michael Halliday's sociocultural account of language see Halliday (2003) 'A brief sketch of systemic grammar', pp. 180–184 and 'Systemic Background', pp. 185–199. For how important the low position of the larynx was, see Leslie Aiello (1998) 'The foundations of human language', pp. 21–34 in Jablonski and Aiello (1998). Regarding the connection and mysteries surrounding Neanderthals, Paul Mellars's 'Neanderthals, modern humans and the archaeological evidence for language' in Jablonski and Aiello (1998) sums up the little we know. Although not directly concerned with language, Stephen Jay Gould's collection of articles on biology and evolution (1977 & 1980) make for a fascinating read. Also not directly concerned with language, but very interesting because of its ecological explanations is Gregory Bateson (2000) 'The role of somatic change in evolution', pp. 346–363. Daniel Dennett (1995), Richard Dawkins (1976) and Steven Pinker (1995) are all bestsellers. All three are excellent, but I particularly enjoyed Dennett's. On Chomsky's position regarding an evolutionary explanation, his Galileo Lecture (2002) 'Perspectives on language and mind', pp. 45–60 is as good a place as any to begin.

Chapter 2: Is Language Exclusive to Humans?

On animal communication, try Peter Marler in Jablonski and Aiello (1998) and Gregory Bateson (2000) 'Redundancy and Coding', pp. 417–431 and 'Metalogue: What is an instinct?', pp. 38–58. Bickerton's first chapter also covers animal communication-systems (1995). Whitehead (1927) is a philosopher and although philosophy does not make for easy reading, this particular book is slim and to the point. On the topic of consciousness there are thousands of books. Bickerton (1995) is a good place to begin reading about this topic's links to language. His opinion on the relation of language to thought is slightly different to the one expressed here, but much closer than many others who assume they are completely separate. Another good book on consciousness is Searle (1994). It provides a background to the main views on consciousness. Although there are few connections made regarding language, if you really want the full picture on consciousness and not just mainstream materialist accounts, the American philosopher William James is the place to go. His '*Principles of Psychology*' (1890, 1957) is a monument to human intelligence. A good, easy-to-read modern account of consciousness is Marvin Minsky (1985). On the modular view of language, there's Trask's chapter 7 (1999) which supports it and is full of useful information. Yule (1996) chapter 15 is cautious about the claims for modules. Ratey (2002) is a well-written account of the holistic view. On how neuroscientists find out what we know about the brain, Loraine K. Obler and Kris Gjerlow's chapter 3 (1999) is very good. The first chapter of the same book also serves as a good introduction to neurolinguistics. Chomsky has written extensively on the relation of mind and language, for example 1968 & 1980. An easy introduction to some of his ideas is Jackendoff (1994). The sociocultural view is presented by Halliday (2003) in chapter 18, 'On language in relation to the evolution of human consciousness'.

Chapter 3: Why Do Languages Change?

There are lots of books on language change. Try Schendl (2001) first. It is brief, but very good. Another place to go is Jean Aitchison

(2001). Next stop is Culpeper (1997): it is very easy to read and has lots of examples of how Old English changed to Middle and Middle to Modern. Many general introductory linguistics text-books include a chapter on this topic. For example, there are Cook's chapter 10 (1997), Fischer's chapter 3 on 'First families' (1999), chapters 19 and 21 in Yule (1996), and Wardhaugh (1993) also has a chapter. On how grammar changes, Joseph Williams's chapters 10 and 11 (1975) offer a generative account. On the history of the English language, there are quite a few non-technical books – Potter (1990) and Burchfield (1985) spring to mind. On the varieties of English, McArthur (1998) is full of information.

Chapter 4: How Does Language Vary across Cultures?

Some aspects covered in this chapter can be found in an easy-to-read format in David Crystal's encyclopaedia (1997a). For a general background to thinking on culture, try Kramsch (1998). There is a wealth of information in the collection of papers written by Jakobson (1990). These papers cover a lot of topics and, though a little dated, they still contain lots of interesting ideas. For those interested in discourse analysis, I suggest Schriffrin (1994). It is detailed, but provides an overview on how the diverse approaches to this subject originated. On Japanese, Miller (1986) is aimed at Japanese linguists, while Makino et al. (1989) is aimed at foreign students of Japanese. On linguistic relativity Sapir (1921 & 1949) are classics and still reward close reading. Whorf (1956), too, is worth reading. Both of these books reveal just how close linguistics was then to the work of anthropologists describing unknown languages. On language universals, Comrie (1981) and Greenberg (1978) give a flavour of the thinking on this subject prior to the rise of generative grammar.

Chapter 5: Where Does Noam Chomsky Fit into Linguistics?

The best short history of linguistics is Robins (1997). But Fischer (1999) chapters 3 and 6 are also useful as a general background to how languages may have developed and multiplied. Randy Harris's aptly titled *The Linguistics Wars* (1993) reconstructs the turbulent sixties and seventies when Chomsky led the struggle to establish his theory. For those interested in Chomsky's minimalist program, try Chomsky (2002) pp. 144–150. An easy introduction to generative thinking is Jackendoff (1994). Two introductions to Chomsky provide useful overviews: one is Belletti and Rizzi's to Chomsky (2002) and another is Hornstein's to the second edition of Chomsky *Rules and Representations* (1980). Both are uncritical and Hornstein's is close to a eulogy.

Chapter 6: How Scientific can Linguistic Theory Be?

On science, I found Okasha (2002) an excellent introduction. For how to judge what is true, I found Quine (1970) and Dancy (1985) very useful. Russell (1912) is also very good. As a background to philosophical issues, Scruton (2004) is a good introduction. On problems facing theorists, Beaugrande (1991) is good. For a clear explanation of the Precede-and-Command Condition and Complex Noun Phrase Constraint rules cited in this chapter, Trask (1999) pp. 31–36 is the place to go. It is technical, but Chomsky (1980) chapter 3 offers insights on how and in what way he believes we will understand language. For additional information on Halliday, I suggest chapter 1 of Halliday (2003).

Chapter 7: What Makes Semantics Difficult?

It is very important to get an overview of approaches to meaning first. The majority approach semantics from one perspective and this can leave students with the impression that it is the only approach. Nöth (1995) does provide an overview that allows you (after a number of readings) to see the wood for the trees. Follow this up with any of the following: Lyons (1995) dense, but very thorough; Hurford and Heasley (1983) the standard university textbook and deservedly so. Not easy, and now rather dated, is Kempson (1977, though revised and last reprinted in 1989). Articles from Wierzbicka (1996) and Frawley (1992) will reward the reader. Now something of a classic is Ogden and Richards (1923). For those who wish to follow meanings' connection to the study of mind, the psychological route, try Lakoff and Johnson (1980). For the sociological route, try Millikan (2005) on conventions or Searle (1995).

Chapter 8: From Whence the Power of Symbols?

For the background on approaches and definitions of 'symbol', Nöth (1995) chapter 2 is a good place to start. Saussure (1916) is a classic and deserves to be read closely, although his conception of the symbol is very different. Peirce's ideas (1966) are the most influential, but he is difficult reading. He has many interpreters, I found Deacon (1997) most useful. On the symbol and society, Derrida (1973 & 1976) and other French writers offer many original insights. Merleau-Ponty (1964) is one example, but Moran (2000) gives useful background on some other thinkers in this tradition – Gadamer, Arendt and Levinas, for example. Foucault (1972) and Lane (2000) on Baudrillard are worth reading. On sociolinguistic thinking regarding language and society, try Williams (1992). On media, try Luhmann (2000).

Chapter 9: How Is Language Represented in the Mind?

Calvin (1996) is a good place to start to get a feel of what's happening in brain research. Then, less focussed on this specific question but very readable, is Ratey (2002). On language from the point of view of philosophers, there is nothing that is very easy. Blackburn (1984) is least difficult. Try comparing Quine (1960) and Chomsky (1980). Wittgenstein (1967) is the most difficult, so it might be best to try one of his many commentators, such as Green (2001) or Fearn (2001). On the third position outlined in this chapter, read James (1912). Guthrie's history of early Greek philosophers provides an excellent background on many philosophical concepts (1962 & 1965).

Bibliography

Aiello, L. C. 1998. 'The Foundations of Human Language.' In N. G. Jablonski & L. C. Aiello (Eds), pp. 21–34, *The Origin and Diversification of Language*. San Francisco: California Academy of Sciences.

Aitchison, Jean. 2001. *Language Change: Progress or Decay?* Cambridge: Cambridge University Press.

Akmajian, Adrian, Richard A. Demers, Ann K. Farmer, and Robert M. Harnish. 1995. *Linguistics: An Introduction to Language and Communication*. Cambridge, Mass.: MIT Press.

Audi, Robert. 1999. *The Cambridge Dictionary of Philosophy* (2nd Edn). R. Audi (Gen. Editor). Cambridge: Cambridge University Press.

Austin, J. L. 1955. *How to Do Things with Words*. Ed. J. O. Urmson & Marian Sbisá. Oxford: Oxford University Press.

Bateson, Gregory. 2000. *Steps to an Ecology of Mind*. Chicago & London: The University of Chicago Press.

Beaugrande, Robert de. 1991. *Linguistic Theory: The Discourse of Fundamental Works*. New York: Longman.

Beichmann, Janine. 2007. 'Through a Glass Darkly: Is Translating Poetry Possible?' in *SWET Newsletter*, Dec., No. 118 pp. 3–20. Tokyo, Japan: Society of Writers, Editors & Translators.

Bickerton, Derek. 1995. *Language and Human Behaviour*. London: UCL Press.

Blackburn, Simon. 1984. *Spreading the Word: Groundings in the Philosophy of Language*. Oxford: Clarendon Press.

Bloomfield, Leonard. (1933) 1950. *Language*. London: George Allen & Unwin Ltd.

Brown, Stuart, Diané Collinson and Robert Wilkinson (Eds). 2002. *Biographical Dictionary of Twentieth-Century Philosophers*. London & New York: Routledge.

Burchfield, Robert. 1985. *The English Language*. Oxford: Oxford University Press.

Bussmann, Hadumod. 1996. *Routledge Dictionary of Language and Linguistics.* Trans. G. P. Trauth & K. Kazzazi. London & New York: Routledge.

Bybee, Joan, Revere Perkins and William Pagliuca. 1994. *The Evolution of Grammar: Tense, Aspect, and Modality in the Languages of the World.* Chicago & London: University of Chicago Press.

Calvin, William H. 1996. *The Cerebral Code: Thinking a Thought in the Mosaics of the Mind.* Cambridge, Mass.: A Bradford Book, The MIT Press.

Cherry, Colin. (1957) 1970. *On Human Communication.* Cambridge, Mass.: MIT Press.

Chomsky, Noam. (1957) 2002. *Syntactic Structures.* The Hague: Mouton.

—1965. *Aspects of the Theory of Syntax.* Cambridge, Mass.: MIT Press.

—(1968) 1972. *Language and Mind.* Enlarged Edition. New York: Harcourt Brace Jovanovich.

—1975. *Reflections on Language.* New York: Pantheon Books.

—(1980) 2005. *Rules and Representations.* New York: Columbia University Press.

—1988. *Language and Problems of Knowledge. The Managua Lectures.* Cambridge, Mass.: The MIT Press.

—2002. *On Nature and Language.* Cambridge: Cambridge University Press.

Comrie, B. 1981. *Language Universals and Linguistic Typology.* Chicago: University of Chicago Press.

Cook, Vivian. 1997. *Inside Language.* London: Arnold.

Coupland, Nikolas, Srikant Sarangi and Christopher N. Candlin (Eds). 2001. *Sociolinguistics and Social Theory.* Harlow, England: Pearson.

Crystal, David. 1995. *The Cambridge Encyclopaedia of The English Language.* Cambridge: Cambridge University Press.

—1997a. *The Cambridge Encyclopaedia of Language* (2nd Edn). Cambridge: Cambridge University Press.

—1997b. *Dictionary of Linguistics and Phonetics.* Oxford: Blackwell.

Culler, Jonathan. 1997. *Literary Theory: A Very Short Introduction.* Oxford & New York: Oxford University Press.

Culpeper, Jonathan. 1997. *History of English.* London & New York: Routledge.

Dancy, Jonathan. 1985. *An Introduction to Contemporary Epistemology.* Oxford: Basil Blackwell.

Davies, Paul. 1998. *The Fifth Miracle: The Search for the Origin of Life.* Bury St. Edmunds, England: Penguin Books.

Dawkins, Richard. (1976) 1989. *The Selfish Gene.* Oxford & New York: Oxford University Press.

—(1982) 1999. *The Extended Phenotype: The Long Reach of the Gene.* Oxford & New York: Oxford University Press.

Deacon, Terrence W. 1997. *The Symbolic Species – The Co-evolution of Language and the Brain.* New York & London: W. W. Norton & Co.

Dennett, Daniel C. 1995. *Darwin's Dangerous Idea: Evolution and the Meanings of Life.* London: Penguin Books.

Derrida, Jacques. 1973. *Speech and Phenomena: And Other Essays on Husserl's Theory of Signs.* Evanston, Ill.: Northwestern University Press.

—1976. *Of Grammatology.* Trans. Gayatri Chakravorty Spivak. Baltimore & London: John Hopkins University Press.

Diamond, Jared. 1999. *Guns, Germs, and Steel – The Fates of Human Societies.* New York & London: W. W. Norton & Co.

Dixon, R. M. W. 1997. *The Rise and Fall of Languages.* Cambridge: Cambridge University Press.

Edwards, P. (Ed. in chief). 1967. *The Encyclopaedia of Philosophy.* (Vol. 4). New York & London: MacMillan Co. & The Free Press.

Emmerich, Michael. 2007. 'Burning the Bridge' in *SWET Newsletter,* June, No. 116 pp. 3–20. Tokyo, Japan: Society of Writers, Editors & Translators.

Fearn, Nicholas. 2001. *Zeno and the Tortoise.* London: Atlantic Books.

Fischer, Steven Roger. 1999. *A History of Language.* London: Reaktion Books.

Foucault, Michel. 1972. *The Archaeology of Knowledge.* New York: Pantheon Books.

Frawley, William. 1992. *Linguistic Semantics.* New Jersey: Lawrence Erlbaum Associates.

Gleick, James. 1998. *Chaos.* London: Vintage.

Gould, Stephen Jay. 1977. *Ever Since Darwin: Reflections in Natural History.* New York & London: W. W. Norton & Co.

—1980. *The Panda's Thumb: More Reflections in Natural History.* New York & London: W. W. Norton & Co.

Green, Karen. 2001. *Dummett: Philosophy of Language.* Cambridge: Polity Press.

Greenberg, J. H. 1963. *Essays in Linguistics.* Chicago: University of Chicago Press.

—1978. *Universals of Human Language. Volume 1: Method and Theory.* Stanford: Stanford University Press.

Guthrie, W. K. C. 1962. *A History of Greek Philosophy. Volume I: The earlier Presocratics and the Pythagoreans.* Cambridge: Cambridge University Press.

—1965. *A History of Greek Philosophy. Volume II: The Presocratic Tradition from Parmenides to Democritus.* Cambridge: Cambridge University Press.

Halliday, M. A. K. 2003. *On Language and Linguistics.* (Vol. 3 in the Collected Works of M. A. K. Halliday. Ed. Jonathan J. Webster). London & New York: Continuum.

Harris, Randy Allen. 1993. *The Linguistics Wars.* New York & Oxford: Oxford University Press.

Hofstede, Geert and G. J. Hofstede. 1991. *Cultures and Organizations – Software for the Mind.* New York: McGraw-Hill.

Hurford, James R. and Brendan Heasley. 1983. *Semantics: A Coursebook.* Cambridge: Cambridge University Press.

Jablonski, N. G. and L. C. Aiello (Eds). 1998. *The Origin and Diversification of Language.* California: University of California Press.

Jackendoff, Ray. 1994. *Patterns in the Mind: Language and Human Nature.* New York: Basicbooks.

Jakobson, Roman. 1990. *On Language.* Ed. L. R. Waugh & M. Monville-Burston. Cambridge: Harvard University Press.

James, William. (1890) 1957. *The Principles of Psychology.* Mineola, New York: Dover Publications Inc.

—(1912) 2003. *Essays in Radical Empiricism.* Mineola, New York: Dover Publications Inc.

—1968. *The Writings of William James: A Comprehensive Edition.* Ed. John McDermott. New York: The Modern Library.

Jenkins, Lyle. 2000. *Biolinguistics: Exploring the Biology of Language.* Cambridge: Cambridge University Press.

Kaku, Michio. 1998. *Visions.* Oxford: Oxford University Press.

Kempson, Ruth M. 1977. *Semantic Theory.* Cambridge: Cambridge University Press.

Kindaichi, Haruhiko. (1957) Translated 1978. *The Japanese Language.* Tokyo, Japan: Charles E. Tuttle Co.

Knight, Chris. 1991. *Blood Relations – Menstruation and the Origins of Culture.* New Haven & London: Yale University Press.

Kramsch, Claire. 1998. *Language and Culture.* Oxford: Oxford University Press.

Lakoff, George and Mark Johnson. 1980. *Metaphors We Live By.* Chicago & London: University of Chicago Press.

Lane, Richard J. 2000. *Jean Baudrillard.* London & New York: Routledge.

Langacker, Ronald W. 2002. *Concept, Image and Symbol.* Berlin: Mouton.

Lévi-Strauss, Claude. 1966. *The Savage Mind.* Chicago: University of Chicago Press.

Luhmann, Niklas. 2000. *The Reality of the Mass Media.* Trans. Kathleen Cross. California: Stanford University Press.

Lyons, John. 1995. *Linguistic Semantics: An Introduction.* Cambridge: Cambridge University Press.

Makino Seichi and Michio Tsutsui. 1989. *A Dictionary of Basic Japanese Grammar.* Tokyo, Japan: The Japan Times.

McArthur, Tom. 1998. *The English Languages.* Cambridge: Cambridge University Press.

Mellars, P. 1998. 'Neanderthals, Modern Humans and the Archaeological Evidence for Language.' In N. G. Jablonski & L. C. Aiello (Eds), pp. 89–115, *The Origin and Diversification of Language.* San Francisco: University of California Press.

Merleau-Ponty, M. 1964. *Signs.* Trans. Richard C. McCleary. Evanston, Ill.: Northwestern University Press.

Miller, R. A. 1986. *Nihongo: in Defence of Japanese.* London: Athlone Press.

Millikan, Ruth Garrett. 2005. *Language: A Biological Model.* Oxford: Clarendon Press.

Minsky, Marvin. 1985. *The Society of Mind.* New York: Simon & Schuster Paperbacks.

Moran, Dermot. 2000. *Introduction to Phenomenology.* London & New York: Routledge.

Nöth, Winfried. 1995. *Handbook of Semiotics*. Bloomington & Indiana: Indiana University Press.

Obler, Loraine K. and Kris Gjerlow. 1999. *Language and the Brain*. Cambridge: Cambridge University Press.

Ogden, C. K. and I. A. Richards. (1923) 1985. *The Meaning of Meaning*. London: Ark Paperbacks.

Okasha, Samir. 2002. *Philosophy of Science*. Oxford: Oxford University Press.

Orwell, George. (1949) 1989. *Nineteen Eighty-Four*. London: Penguin Books.

Peirce, Charles S. (1958) 1966. *Charles S. Peirce: Selected Writings. (Values in a Universe of Chance)*. Ed. Philip P. Wiener. New York: Dover Publications.

Pinker, Steven. 1995. *The Language Instinct – How the Mind Creates Language*. New York: HarperPerennial.

—1998. 'The Evolution of the Human Language Faculty.' In N. G. Jablonski & L. C. Aiello (Eds), pp. 117–126, *The Origin and Diversification of Language*. San Francisco: University of California Press.

Potter, Simeon. 1990. *Our Language*. Harmondsworth, England: Penguin.

Quine, W. v. O. 1960. *Word and Object*. Cambridge, Mass.: MIT Press.

Quine, W. v. O. and J. S. Ullian. 1970. *The Web of Belief*. New York: Random House.

Quirk, Randolph, Sidney Greenbaum, Geoffrey Leech and Jan Svartvik. 1985. *A Comprehensive Grammar of the English Language*. London & New York: Longman.

Ratey, J. J. 2002. *A User's Guide to the Brain. Perception, Attention, and the Four Theaters of the Brain*. New York: Vintage Books.

Robins, R. H. 1997. *A Short History of Linguistics*. London & New York: Longman.

Russell, Bertrand. (1912) 2001. *The Problems of Philosophy*. Oxford: Oxford University Press.

Sanders, Andrew. 1994. *The Short Oxford History of English Literature* (3rd Edn). Oxford: Oxford University Press.

Sapir, Edward. 1921. *Language: An Introduction to the Study of Speech*. New York: Harcourt Brace.

—1949. *Selected Writings of Edward Sapir in Language, Culture, and Personality.* Ed. David G. Mandelbaum. California: University of California Press.

Saussure, Ferdinand de. (1916) 1969. *Course in General Linguistics.* Trans. Wade Baskin. New York: McGraw-Hill.

Schendl, Herbert. 2001. *Historical Linguistics.* Oxford: Oxford University Press.

Schiffrin, Deborah. 1994. *Approaches to Discourse.* Oxford, U.K. & Cambridge, Mass.: Blackwell.

Scruton, Roger. 2004. *Modern Philosophy: An Introduction and Survey.* London: Pimlico.

Searle, John R. 1992. *The Rediscovery of the Mind.* Cambridge, Mass.: MIT Press.

—1995. *The Construction of Social Reality.* New York: The Free Press.

—1998. *Mind, Language and Society: Philosophy in the Real World.* New York: Basic Books.

Sebeok, Thomas A. 1994. *Signs: An Introduction to Semiotics.* Toronto, Canada: University of Toronto Press.

Sharpe, Peter. 2002. 'The Origins of Language.' In 語学研究 (Language Study) No. 99, pp. 29–50. Tokyo, Japan: Takushoku University Press.

—2003. 'Linguistic Diversity.' In 語学研究 (Language Study) No. 102, pp. 1–26. Tokyo, Japan: Takushoku University Press.

—2004a. 'Language and Consciousness.' In 語学研究 (Language Study) No. 105, pp. 1–30. Tokyo, Japan: Takushoku University Press.

—2004b. 'Language and Culture.' In 語学研究 (Language Study) No. 106, pp. 24–50. Tokyo, Japan: Takushoku University Press.

—2004c. 'Language and Semiotics.' In 語学研究 (Language Study) No. 107, pp. 71–101. Tokyo, Japan: Takushoku University Press.

—2005a. 'Language and Linguistics.' In 語学研究 (Language Study) No. 108, pp. 43–75. Tokyo, Japan: Takushoku University Press.

—2005b. 'Language and Philosophy.' In 語学研究 (Language Study) No. 109, pp. 159–193. Tokyo, Japan: Takushoku University Press.

—2006. 'Symbolic Signs.' In 語学研究 (Language Study) No. 113, pp. 19–43. Tokyo, Japan: Takushoku University Press.

Taylor, John R. 2002. *Cognitive Grammar.* New York: Oxford University Press.

Thompson, Mel. 2001. *Philosophy of Mind.* London: Teach Yourself.

Trask, R. L. 1999a. *Key Concepts in Language and Linguistics.* London: Routledge.

—1999b. *Language: The Basics* (2nd Edn). London: Routledge.

Trefil, James. 2001. *Encyclopedia of Science and Technology.* James Trefil (Gen. Editor). New York & London: Routledge.

Wardhaugh, Ronald. 1993. *Investigating Language. Central Problems in Linguistics.* Oxford: Blackwell.

Whitehead, Alfred North. (1927) 1985. *Symbolism: Its Meaning and Effect.* New York: Fordham University Press.

Whorf, B. L. 1956. *Language, Thought and Reality: Selected Writings of Benjamin Lee Whorf.* Ed. John B. Carroll. Cambridge, Mass.: MIT Press.

Widdowson, Henry G. 1996. *Linguistics.* Oxford: Oxford University Press.

Wierzbicka, Anna. 1996. *Semantics – Primes and Universals.* Oxford & New York: Oxford University Press.

Williams, Glyn. 1992. *Sociolinguistics: A Sociological Critique.* London & New York: Routledge.

Williams, Joseph M. 1975. *Origins of the English Language: A Social and Linguistic History.* New York: The Free Press.

Winston, Robert and Don E. Wilson. 2004. *Smithsonian Human.* New York: Dorley Kindersley Ltd.

Wittgenstein, Ludwig. 1967. *Philosophical Investigations.* Trans. Elizabeth G. M. Anscombe, (3rd Edn). Oxford: Blackwell.

Yule, George. 1996. *The Study of Language.* Cambridge: Cambridge University Press.

Index

Boas, Franz 92, 102–3
Bopp, Franz 100
brain
    electrochemical activity in
        199–201
    increase in size of 9–12
    language as module in 43–50
    language faculty in 109, 119,
        126
    layers of 10
    mental representation and
        199–201
    organization of language
        in 210–15
    plasticity 44
brain expansion 9–12
brain function 47–8
brain size
    of early hominids 7
Broca, Paul 45
Brugmann, Karl 101
brute facts 188
Bussman, Hadumod 118

Calvin, William 200, 201
The Canterbury Tales (Chaucer) 54
Cartesian theory of mind 164–5
case inflections 55, 70–3
Categorical Grammar 117–18
categorization 167–8
causation xii
cave art 14
Caxton, Will 61
Celtic languages 57
chance events
    language change and 62–3,
        69–70

Charron, Pierre 208
Chaucer, Geoffrey 54
children
    concept formation in 177
    deaf 1
    innateness hypothesis and 107–9
    language acquisition by 1, 44–5,
        95
    maternal investment in 16
chimpanzees 3–4, 37
Chinese 156
Chomsky, Noam 42, 47, 98
    background of 105
    on concept of language 123
    influences on 99–105
    innateness hypothesis 107–9,
        118
    on internalist theory 134–7,
        142–4
    on language faculty 109, 126,
        153–4
    legacy of 119–21
    on linguistics as natural
        science 145
    Logical Structure of Linguistic
        Theory 106
    on origins of language 1–2, 21
    on semantics 170
    standard theory of 109–12
    syntactic movement 115–16
    Syntactic Structures 106, 107
    tranformational-generative
        (T-G) grammar 106–7
classicism 99
code-switching 88–9
cognition 220–1
cognitive abilities